A Startup Life

A Novel

Bob Fisher

CHAPTER 1

Sometimes, it's just guts.

Following through on the dream of making that long-planned, life-changing move. It begins as an embryonic concept before becoming enhanced and idealized. Later, it evolves into an aspiration, then a mission, and finally, a hunger. But the actual dream seems to forever be three steps away. Always some reason this is not the right time. The dream is useless if you're still on the hamster wheel. John Victor finally believed the cycle had gone on too long and had really become a matter of intestinal fortitude. So, one day last April, he surprised everyone, including himself, by accepting the risk and taking the plunge.

It is now June, 2004. It has been two months since John

shocked his fellow colleagues and his former employer by turning in his resignation. His associates considered John at the top of his game and wondered, why in the world would he leave now? And by all accounts, his rise at Aurelian Software over the past six years was indeed stellar; spanning tech management, followed by marketing and sales, and eventually, being put in charge of company-wide strategic planning. The new business unit he had created within Aurelian was growing like a weed, with the peak of his success coming from a novel new product he launched, which had quickly gained a following. The product facilitated inter-company transactions, such as purchase orders, and had found its audience, soon becoming a significant revenue stream for his division.

John's decision at age 28 to walk away from the momentum his new product was gaining and bootstrap his own company was more of an act of passion than the rational choice many had come to expect from him. Even so, he and his wife, Lynn, had rejoiced in the change and celebrated this new life chapter.

It is now late June and John has been laying out the business plans for his new company, the eponymously named Victech LLC—while waiting for his co-founder to join him full time. As he makes the critical phone call, he begins to question the rationality of his bold move for the first time.

When Russ picks up, John cuts to the chase. "We doing this or not?"

"Good morning to you too, John."

"Have you given notice yet?"

"I'm getting my office set up at home. These things can't be rushed, you know."

He hasn't given notice. The stalling is just too much. "Please cast your memory back to our agreed-upon plan," John says, launching his tongue-in-cheek oration. "It was many months ago, but you may recollect we agreed to quit our day jobs and pursue this thing together. Full time. I believe we agreed your role is to lead product development, not parking yourself in some partner-in-waiting purgatory."

"It hasn't been that long—"

"The bottom line is, it's past time for product development to get started. I need you to join me in the unbridled joy of putting twelve-hour days into this thing." He pauses, sensing that Russ may actually be fearful of pulling the plug on his salaried job as John had. He needs reassurance. Best to tone down the rhetoric. "Come-on, Russ. Let's do this. Wealth and fame are surely right around the corner. Plus, you'll have gobs of fun achieving them."

"How long did you say we'll have to go without a paycheck?" Russ asks.

John does not appreciate Russ' deflection, vaguely insinuating that his co-founder is not already committed, but he chooses to ignore it rather than provoke Russ. He cannot risk him going entirely off the rails. John's strategy at this stage is to proceed in accordance with his First Lesson of Startups: Build, Don't Spend. Of course, having income will become a necessity at some point, so he had already worked up a pro forma spreadsheet for the new company. Like most pre-launch business models, the attempt to project sales growth and cash-flow from a non-existent product, using non-existent staff, working out of a non-existent office contains enough unknown variables to yield any desired answer with a minimal amount of tweaking. Garbage in, garbage out. Such is the nature of computer models.

John responds that he hopes they will be able to pay themselves some sort of salary within nine months. Russ listens without comment as John walks through the key assumptions, taking some comfort from the knowledge that John has apparently thought this through. In calmer tones than before, the conversation drifts into talk of the next steps each of them needs to take in the upcoming weeks to maximize progress.

"Just let me know when you have given your notice," John says, winding up the call.

"Sure, John. Be sure to call me hourly."

After disconnecting, John reflects on his choice of Russ as Victech's co-founder especially in light of their history. Russell McGraw had worked for John as a software developer during John's early days as a manager at Aurelian. John recalls the protests from Lynn at dinner one night when he first informed her he planned to tap Russ as co-founder.

"Russ McGraw? The guy you said never makes deadlines? The guy who's never able to estimate how long anything will take? Why would you want to rely on him to develop your first products?"

"Two reasons," John had replied. "First, I know from our prior collaboration he will eventually deliver high-quality code. Secondly, he is one of very few people I know willing to take the risk of working without a paycheck to get this thing started."

"So, in the meantime, it's okay if he puts you through living hell?"

"Babe, this is a new and unfunded company so, yes, those criteria trump all else. At least for now."

CHAPTER 2

Lynn already regrets the visit.

Marsha Nagless lured her daughter to her house on the pretext of asking for her help planning a trip with Lynn's father. But the conversation soon reveals the ruse.

"Your father and I just want to know – why did he leave his job?"

I should have seen this coming; Lynn thinks. The real objective is to harangue me once again over John's career move, not to help plan a trip. Let the rant begin. "Are we really doing this again, Mom? We've already had this conversation. Must I explain once again that John's lifelong ambition has always been to build his own company?"

"But at his old company, he was well paid and could support both of you. He was moving up. Now – where will your income come from? How can you start a family with no income?"

There it is. Lynn wished she had never shared the news that she and John were trying to get pregnant. It became one more bludgeon for her mother to use along with the implication that Lynn's part-time work as a travel agent will not cover their bills. Which was obviously true but not appreciated.

Lynn fumes as her mother prattles on: "I don't understand what you're thinking. You know your father and I cannot support you any longer…"

"No one is asking you to, mother!" Lynn says, suddenly triggered. "We can take care of ourselves. When are you going to show any sort of confidence in John or me that we know what the fuck we are doing?"

"Don't be coarse, dear. It's just that we have seen young couples take a wrong turn and struggle for years. We cannot just sit by and watch while you two get yourselves into trouble."

"I'm twenty-three, mother. John and I have been

married for over a year. We are adults and have every right to get ourselves into trouble. And to be fucking coarse too."

The conversation degenerates further. After ten more minutes of getting nowhere, Lynn storms out of the house in silence. She backs her car down the driveway, aims it toward the main street, and tears down the open road replaying the scathing words in her head. As if we had even asked her to support us, Lynn thinks. While Lynn's father keeps his own counsel, Marsha always seems to target Lynn's hot buttons. Driving home, her thoughts return to the first time she and John discussed her mother's bluntness. Lynn had asked John what *his* mother thinks. He had lost his father in early childhood, but John's mother was still ever-present and usually a source of candor.

"And what does your mother say about the job change?" she had asked him.

John had grinned: "She says my father would have been very proud."

Lynn certainly harbored her own concerns about family income prior to John's resignation from Aurelian. He did not seem especially preoccupied with the risk, though, for when she had posed the question of their finances, he only laughed and said: "You and I must gather nuts for the long Winter ahead."

No real answers, but also, no hint of concern. Unlike her mother, Lynn has confidence in John and his ability to make this new venture work somehow. Even so, she worries about money more than she lets on. The path that lies ahead is anything but clear.

CHAPTER 3

It is September 2006. It has been more than two years since John guesstimated he and Russ would have paychecks within nine months. That is ancient history: there has been no compensation for the founders to date, nor is any visible on the horizon. However, Victech did launch its first product: a testing tool to help implement the exchange of intercompany transactions. This is another aspect of the business automation process John first worked with at Aurelian although the new Victech product does not overlap or compete with those of his former employer. Victech has made several initial sales of the product to prestigious Fortune companies and the company has generated actual revenue, albeit modestly so far. To pay for office space and a few contractors who comprise the makeshift programming and support team, the company's initial funding came largely from the founders themselves with some additional contributions from supportive family members.

On this cool crisp Fall morning, John and Russ walk around the office park in Dublin Ohio which houses dozens of small companies including Victech. Central Ohio's beautiful autumns are notoriously short with trees already shedding their most radiant colors. This walk has become the preferred venue for most company meetings and John takes the opportunity to inform Russ that their existing funds can provide only the shortest of runways.

The unwelcome news: they need to hire fulltime sales staff, further postponing salaries for the founders. To date, the company had only retained a handful of contractors with John functioning as both CEO and Sales department.

Russ is nonplussed: "How do we afford that? If we increase our burn rate, we'll just go bankrupt sooner."

John bristles at Russ's choice of words although he realizes the assessment is not entirely irrational. "Second Lesson of Startups: Success Burns Through Money Faster. We have a few sales and a decent pipeline. But we need to raise money to get ahead of the curve. It requires fulltime Sales Reps. We'll never cut it with just me selling in my copious spare time."

"Along those lines, John, I also have some breaking news," Russ responds. "My former employer has extended an offer to me which is too good to refuse. I have decided to accept."

John is stunned. He slows his stride before coming to a full stop. "You're bailing on me?"

Russ faces him. "Look, I need the money. I have a family and expenses. You have Ernie, now. He can do it without me."

Ernie Chase is one of two young software developers Victech brought on board as contractors, along with one contracted support person. It was Ernie who completed the bulk of the new product development in record time. Both John and Russ were amazed by his efficiency. Powered by a seemingly unlimited quantity of Red Bull and donning his ever-present headphones, the twenty-two-year-old is a software programming dynamo.

"If you are really gone, I agree Ernie is the one to lead product development," says John, sighing. "I really am sorry for the squeeze you must be under, and I'm sorry if it has come to this."

Russ would stay on for three more weeks, turning over his work product and plans to Ernie. During that time, John and Russ agreed to separation terms which include Russ surrendering most of his founder's stock and a schedule for Victech to repay Russ most of his capital investment in Victech.

John also extended a full-time salaried offer to Ernie as Lead Developer who graciously accepted it on the spot.

"Cool. Thanks, dude," Ernie said grinning, before once again disappearing into his computer screen and headphones.

Clearly a man of few words, notes John.

The larger looming issue, of course, is the mounting pressure to find and secure a new funding source. In addition to the need for full-time Sales and Ernie's increased salary, John is feeling the pinch. This is especially true since John is now within several months of becoming a first-time father, piling onto the financial and temporal demands of keeping his on-the-edge bootstrap company alive.

CHAPTER 4

In late 2006, Angel funding of start-ups is in its early days, and Venture Capital activity is still largely confined to Silicon Valley and Boston. However, John's friend, Tim Weathers, is a freelance lawyer who set up Victech as an LLC, and since then, he has unofficially taken the role of its part-time general counsel. Recently, Tim offered to introduce John to a potential funding source.

"This guy, Jeffrey Brown, is a senior partner in the Ripley Davidson Hopewell law firm," Tim explains. John knew Tim had made this connection through his networking and involvement in civic projects for the city of Columbus, and he was familiar with Ripley Davidson from its reputation as one of Ohio's largest legal firms. "Jeffrey is making noise about an investment group he's starting. He has a vision of leading investment in local start-ups by tapping his network of lawyers and wealthy clients."

"How many deals has this group done?" John asked.

Tim smiles. "I suspect you'll be his first."

***

The next day, Tim makes a persuasive email introduction of John to Jeffrey, leading to a brief conference call with the three of them. Afterward, they agree John and Tim will visit Jeffrey at Ripley Davidson's offices the following week, and John will make his pitch in person.

It is now Tuesday, Tim and John arrive at Ripley Davidson headquarters. The office is a sprawling affair located in a sixty-year-old building in downtown Columbus. The décor inside features elegant, traditional oak paneling as far as the eye can see. A tall and comely female, who introduces herself as Joan, formally greets them at the front desk and leads them through a maze of hallways ending in a conference room lined floor-to-ceiling with voluminous legal prints.

Jeffrey appears and greets Tim warmly, extending his hand, "It's great to see you again, Tim. I really appreciate you bringing me into this exciting opportunity."

"It's my pleasure, Jeffrey," Tim responds. "Allow me to introduce our man of the hour. Jeffrey Brown, please meet John Victor."

"Nice to meet you, Mr. Victor. I am looking forward to learning more about your great company, Victech."

"Thanks, Jeffrey," John replies. "Happy to fill you in."

John had imagined he would be meeting an older man. While Jeffrey's speech is slow and halting, John estimates the man shaking his hand to be in his early fifties—not in his seventies as he'd have guessed from the phone call. Jeffrey's voice and demeanor belie his age. John wonders if spending one's life isolated in this dense jungle of law books adds hard miles. Some people just seem to be born to be old, John thinks.

Joan emerges at the conference room door with a helper pushing a cart bearing coffee and fresh pastries. As the three men help themselves to the food and settle into their chairs, John begins his pitch by citing his own background, starting with his education and early exposure to technology, including computer programming. He explains how, at Aurelian, he applied his skills to inter-company commerce, a field which actually predates consumer electronic commerce. His story culminates with his success and growth at Aurelian and his desire to start his own company, which became Victech. For the next fifteen minutes, John describes how Victech will bring fresh innovation into this field. In winding up his presentation, John states, "In summary, this is a simple concept in a young field in which there are no other existing solutions."

Tim gives John a thumbs up and turns to Jeffrey, who is smiling ear to ear. It has become apparent he is smitten with John and his concept. "This sounds fantastic, John! Exactly the type of Central Ohio based small business my investors are seeking." Jeffrey proposes that John meets his full investment group in the near future, and John agrees. The meeting ends shortly after with handshakes and warm 'thanks' all around.

Walking back to the car, John confides in Tim, "I'm not sure how well Jeffrey understood our business model. What do you think?"

"I think it doesn't matter. Your enthusiasm is contagious. Jeffrey doesn't need to understand the product or market—he wants to be a star deal maker. The only important thing is that he believes you are the guy that will make it happen."

CHAPTER 5

Tim's assessment soon proves accurate. Within ten days, Jeffrey assembles a group of early investors. Most of them are Ripley Davidson lawyers, but the lot also includes some high-net-worth locals. Over the next two weeks, John will give a series of similar pitches to many of them in response to their requests. The signup is progressing.

Concurrently, Jeffrey and John are exchanging emails to flesh out the terms of the investment. It will be a $2.5 million infusion consisting of two-thirds debt and one-third equity. There are twenty-eight investors in total, including Jeffrey. The detailed terms will soon be shared in a massive agreement, which John assumes has been drafted by an army of Ripley Davidson lawyers at stratospheric billing rates. Noteworthy among the terms is a put option that gives each investor the right to require the company to buy back their equity shares, should they exercise the option after five years. Tim explains to John that investors use such options to assure themselves a way of cashing out of the investment if an exit does not occur quickly enough. Since companies are often not able to buy out their investors' stakes, put options are sometimes used as leverage to wrest control from the founders and replace the CEO. John tells Tim that Victech has no plans to go there—ever.

John has had little experience with the dense legalese in the memorandum, so he calls Jeffrey several times with questions about some of the more obscure wording. Jeffrey's patience for these calls soon wears thin. It is clear Jeffrey wants to be the trusted big daddy, and he bristles at John's scrutiny. "John, you need to spend your time building Victech and not getting caught up in these details. I frankly cannot believe you are reading all of that."

Sensing Jeffrey's growing impatience, John attempts to calm the waters. "Jeffrey, I just need to understand the respective commitments of both parties. I'm not trying to question anyone's trustworthiness."

"You don't need to worry about it. Sign it, and go build your company."

Having no alternative source of available funding, John silently concludes Jeffrey's instructions sound like a plan, as this is his only plan. As the call ends, he mentally notes the Third Lesson of Startups: Sometimes The Only Choice Is The Right Choice. That's either profound or a truism, he thinks. I really ought to write these down someday.

Jeffrey again proves good to his word, and John receives a check for the full investment in November. With the new funds, Victech proceeds to hire its first sales team. John begins to draw a salary under the frugal investor terms. Even though it is less than half of what John had been making at Aurelian, it does help reduce the distraction of worrying about money. For now.

***

The modest paycheck brings great relief to the Victor household and just in time for Baby Maddy's first Christmas. Madison Marie Victor had been born two weeks earlier. John and Lynn interpret the timing variously.

"We'll save a ton on gifts by combining her birthday and Christmas each year," is John's takeaway.

Lynn sees it differently. "It's a giant rip off, and she'll know it and blame us when she gets older. The savings will be eaten up by future therapy costs."

John grins. "Love it. So, we agree to disagree?"

"I can't go along with that."

"OK—we disagree to disagree," John shrugs, and they both laugh. John lights the wood in the fireplace as Lynn nurses little Maddy. "Speaking of our newborn, it seems your mom now heads the Baby Maddy Fan Club. How are you guys getting along?"

"We're really good right now. The baby brings out the best in her. Since the delivery, she has been one-hundred-percent supportive. Apparently, we now have a volunteer baby sitter twenty-four-seven, and the price is right. It also doesn't hurt that I mentioned you're finally getting a paycheck."

"Don't tell your parents how small it is—we don't want your mom reverting."

The flames lick the walls of the firebox. The exhausted couple sits on the floor near the Christmas tree and study Maddy's tiny face.

"She's a little cutie, ain't she?" asks John.

"Gorgeous. Almost makes it worth it that we'll never have a good night's sleep again."

CHAPTER 6

In October of 2011, it has been almost five years since the group led by Jeffrey Brown invested in Victech.

Marcus Mitchell takes a seat in the chair across from John's desk. The African American man is on the shorter side and has a pleasant, round face and an energetic smile. John puts the man's age as early thirties.

"Nice to meet you, Marcus," John welcomes his guest. "I understand you are sort of a freelance Human Resource pro?"

"That's a fair way to put it. Sometimes called a fractional H.R. Director. Nice meeting you too."

"Could you tell me a bit about your typical H.R. stint?"

"Happy to. I was a full-time H.R. Director with a local company here in town for the past five years before it was acquired by a Boston-based firm last year. I am a SHRM Certified Professional. SHRM is the world's largest H.R. membership organization, and I hold the only type of H.R. certification they offer. My experience spans the gamut of Human Resources. Of late, most of my projects have been for local start-ups trying to establish office policies and optimizing employee benefits. Naturally, always within tight budget constraints."

"Office policies and benefits are definitely areas requiring experienced guidance," John nods. "How are you with personnel issues?"

"I've seen it all." He pauses, then says, "This conversation is confidential. What have you got?"

I thought you'd never ask, John thinks. He describes the situation, silently praying it does not scare Marcus off. "Mabel Denning was our first office manager. Among her responsibilities was the hiring and management of a small admin staff. Over a stretch of five months, she hired, and subsequently fired, three different individuals as combined receptionist and secretary for our office's front-desk position."

"Wow, okay. Got it. Sounds like Mabel could use some coaching on best hiring practices," Marcus says.

"Hang on," says John. "It gets much worse. Last month, Mabel hired a lady, named Sarah, for this position. Almost immediately, the friction began. Sarah typically arrives five to ten minutes late, which is meticulously recorded by Mabel. In Mabel's view, Sarah is unkempt, her desk is a mess, she has a bad attitude, and her phone skills are unprofessional."

"Do you agree with those assessments?"

John shrugs, "Not especially. I should probably explain at this point that the culture here at Victech is somewhat laissez faire. Not chaotic, but informal enough to make everyone feel relaxed and hopefully appreciated. But there was something about Sarah which drew out the authoritarian in Mabel."

"So, Sarah becomes the fourth fired receptionist?"

"Yes, but this time, it doesn't end there. After firing Sarah, Mabel became unglued. She literally chased Sarah out the door, yelling at the girl, cursing her, and telling her she is scum and will never amount to anything. Effectively, she threatened her and Sarah's future livelihood."

Marcus' jaw drops. "Seriously? Unbelievable! Where are

we now? Is Mabel still here?"

"I let her go as soon as I found out. The issue now is Sarah."

"You expect her to sue?"

"Sure—but even if she doesn't, I want the damage to be undone and Victech's name cleared. We just don't operate this way. Sarah will not take my calls right now. I need help in making this right."

John and Marcus formulate a plan of action that includes Marcus acting as the middle man. He agrees to contact Sarah and extend apologies on behalf of the company. He will also present Sarah with a written reference from Victech's CEO and assist her in finding new employment.

When they have settled on the details, John says, "Marcus, this is clearly a very short-term project. I want you to know that if you and I decide we enjoy working together, we have no shortage of other queued projects that I believe can benefit from your expertise."

Marcus laughs. "I would hope they are not all crises of this hair-on-fire variety."

"Of course not," says John. "But there's no shortage of those either."

Two weeks later, Sarah has graciously accepted the apology and written reference, and successfully landed a job of similar stature. At the same time, Marcus accepts the full-time position as Victech's first H.R. Director.

CHAPTER 7

The CFO, Marianne Lowe, catches John as he attempts to bolt from the conference room following the product meeting. He was hoping to avoid her today, but she is too quick to permit his escape.

"A moment of your time, please?" she asks, waving him back into the room.

"Sure," says John, as the others depart the room.

As they filter out, Marianne closes the door and jumps to the point, "Two weeks from today is the date."

John nods. He already knew the date, but thus far, has chosen to not focus on it.

"Any idea how many will pull the trigger?" she asks.

"No—I need to reach out to Jeffrey and have him give us a whip count. How many can we afford?"

Marianne ponders momentarily. "Maybe a handful. Not many more. You need to contact Jeffrey soon. Like, yesterday."

"Will do." John nods again and heads back towards his office. This cannot be put off. Reaching his desk, he finds an email from Marianne. It consists of a popular meme featuring a creepy-looking cat and the word "SOON."

"Yes, dear," John types in response.

Victech had a sluggish start, but the 2006 infusion from Jeffrey's investor group allowed the company to hire a sales team and reinvest in its early growth. That was five years ago and the company has now secured a dozen Fortune clients and is making strong progress forward. But growing start-ups gobble up cash fast, and the company is not close to being able to fund the stock buy-back should most of the investors exercise their put option. John is hopeful that Jeffrey's investors will understand this and not want to bankrupt the rapidly growing company.

John places the call to Jeffrey, who listens attentively as John advances the case why the put should not be exercised at this time. At the end, John asks Jeffrey how many investors he thinks are inclined to exercise this option. Jeffrey admits he has no idea and that his investment group has not met for over a year. They agree the best way forward will be to convene an all-investors meeting in which John can review the company's progress and make a bullish case for the company's future.

CHAPTER 8

After so many years of casual dress, John has grown unaccustomed to traditional suit-and-tie attire. As he mingles with his investors in the social hour prior to his presentation, it's obvious his choice of garb—or more precisely, Lynn's choice of his garb—was correct. After all, these are partners and other assorted senior lawyers from a stodgy old-school law firm. Anything less than formal would not have reflected well on John or Victech. And now, five days before the investors are able to exercise enough of their put options to drive Victech into default—John is acutely aware that his performance tonight is a do-or-die matter. Glad there's no pressure, he notes to himself.

He spots Lyra Keller, Victech's Marketing Director, approaching from across the room. She really rises to the occasion, John thinks. No surprise. Lyra is always appropriately dressed for business, but tonight, clad in an elegant black dress, she is more stunning than usual. She has been schmoozing the investors for the best part of the hour. The old men all relish making small talk with this gorgeous creature. She engages them in congenial conversation and humor, occasionally interjecting a raunchy ad lib for shock value.

Lyra notices that the open bar has been doing healthy business all night. She steps away from the investors, so they're out of earshot, and closer to John. "Do we want them liquored up?" Lyra whispers.

John grins. "Just feeling good. We still need them to be coherent."

"Based on the discussions I've had around this room, that may be a high bar."

"You've had some interesting exchanges?"

"Why, yes—see the gent over there in the three-piece suit? The one who resembles a warmed-over cadaver? I attempted to engage him by expounding on the value of Victech's unique market positioning. In turn, he tells me I remind him of Jayne Mansfield while he stares nonstop at my chest."

John stifles his laugh. "So, you found the conversation less than productive?"

She scoffs. "Par for the course. When does this thing actually get underway?"

On cue, at the far end of the room, Jeffrey announces that it's time for attendees to take their seats.

"Break a leg," Lyra says as John heads to the front.

As the investors settle in, John takes the podium.

"I appreciate you all for coming to this update meeting. My team and I are delighted to announce that your company is currently experiencing the best growth momentum in its history. I would like to take a few minutes tonight to describe our recent sales successes, the growing market acceptance of Victech solutions, our new annual recurring revenue high watermark, and our robust sales and product pipelines."

John begins his slide show that will consume the next twenty minutes. With years of practice at public speaking, John is able to engage his audience and get a sense of their receptivity. This comes in the form of assorted nods and grunts of appreciation as he cites individual customer successes and indicators of the market's growing awareness of Victech. The last slide references the five-year anniversary of their investment, and John uses it to reinforce his messages of growth and success.

He then tackles the issue of the put option head-on but adroitly avoids detailing the company's inability to finance a mass exodus should most of them exercise their option.

"You will soon have a choice to make regarding your own individual investment, and I would urge you not to exit the company at this time. You have seen our excellent momentum and trajectory tonight. Buying back shares of our stock is not a good use of company capital, which is better deployed in feeding our growth." John thanks them all for coming and steps down from the stage where several investors promptly corner him with questions and comments about the update. After a few minutes, they disperse into the thronged group of attendees talking amongst themselves near the bar. It appears no one is leaving the meeting room.

John seeks out Lyra across the room and makes his way over to her. Among her skills, John knows she is perceptive and has the ability to read the room in an insightful and nuanced way.

"Well, how did we do?" he asks upon reaching her, taking her aside.

Lyra has her line ready. "You crushed it, boss. Any better and they'd be stuffing dollar bills into your belt!"

"High praise indeed. Now, tell me what you're really sensing in this room."

"Not entirely sure. I am getting mixed signals, both excitement and consternation, which is difficult to interpret. There is clearly some sort of problem."

***

Following John's presentation the previous night, Jeffrey had promised to poll his group and let John know how many members are likely to exercise their put option by today. John has spent the majority of his Friday morning awaiting his call, when finally, it comes through around lunchtime.

"Hi, John. It's Jeffrey. The group is very impressed with the company growth, but the put option requires each of us to make a choice whether to have Victech buy us out."

"Your group all sees our momentum, Jeffrey. We're doing great. Why would anyone want to exit at this time?"

"Many in my group do not want to, but this is the only guaranteed liquidity opportunity built into our agreement. Most are troubled that there is no assurance of an exit after this put option expires."

And whose fault is that? John thinks. Your genius lawyers put this deal together—I just agreed to it. After a heart-stopping moment and lingering silence, the problem has become painfully clear. Are a bunch of these investors really going to exercise their put option? John needs to buy some time to think through his response.

"Jeffrey, I hear you and understand. Give us the weekend, and we'll propose a course of action to address your group's concerns."

CHAPTER 9

John plays racquetball with Tim Weathers most Saturday mornings. Outside of his business role as legal counsel for Victech, they have become good friends. As a trusted confidant, Tim is able to balance legal and business considerations, making John eager to discuss the put issue with him; not only for his advice, but as someone who is neither an employee nor an investor in Victech, he knows that Tim's perspective will be free of either bias. But at the moment, John is unleashing pent-up stress on the court, violently lashing out at the ball.

Tim calls him out on it after John muffs an easy lob shot before crashing into a wall.

"I didn't bring my chain mail armor today. What is with you?"

Breathlessly John responds: "We need to talk. When you're done pounding me on this court, let me buy you breakfast."

"Alright, but we really need to discuss switching to Pickleball."

***

Cucos Taqueria, in Upper Arlington, is one of their longtime favorites after racquetball. Over coffee on the patio, John replays the investor meeting, including the put issue and Jeffrey's explanation of the investors' concerns.

Tim listens thoughtfully and then offers: "Put options are often used to gain control of a company that's missing its goals. But in this case, Jeffrey's group just wants an escape hatch. It sounds like they want an additional exit opportunity after this one."

"Who doesn't?" John responds. "We want them to be aligned with the company—not pressuring us to take them out at some arbitrary future date where the timing could be even worse. No. I don't want to provide them another fixed exit option."

"Well, you can't change the current option they have. It is theirs. Their choice is all-or-nothing."

Tim's response gives John pause. The two sit silently for several minutes.

John then replies, "Maybe... that is the key."

"Not following. What do you mean?"

"Well, there's nothing stopping us from adding to their available choices."

With his eyebrows raised, Tim asks, "Such as?"

"Maybe some sort of partial put option: allow them to retain a piece of their equity and give us an easier timeline for paying off the balance."

Tim is immediately on it. Over the next hour, they navigate through the construction of a new alternative to provide Jeffrey. They frame it as a half-and-half put option. The original put remains available to the investors as-is for those who choose it, but for those selecting the new "HAH" put, the Company will buy back half of their stock, starting now, with payments spread over five years with simple interest, effectively making it become new debt. With their remaining equity, the HAH investors will retain a stake in the growing company while gaining enough guaranteed liquidity that their investment has already been fully repaid. As Tim puts it: "Everyone likes to play with house money."

They bang out a letter to Jeffrey describing the key terms of the HAH put option and eagerly wait for his response.

***

During the Monday afternoon debriefing, John has assembled the Victech senior staff. When they are gathered, John delivers the news. "So, Jeffrey called me after he reviewed the HAH put to say he was thrilled."

The conference room erupts into rowdy applause and whoo-hoo shouts.

John waits for the room to simmer before continuing, "He pointed out that it puts his investors in the black and allows them to retain a stake in our future. Somewhere deep down in his priority list, he may also recognize that it saves the company from default."

There is light laughter and more applause from the staff.

After it gets quiet again, Marianne chimes in: "He'll probably take credit for coming up with the idea, though."

John shrugs. "He is welcome to it. Especially if it helps him sell it to the group."

* * *

While John's persuasive presentation had teed up excitement about the company's momentum, it is the HAH alternative that sends the investor buy-in over the top. Of the twenty-eight original outside investors, twenty-five select the new option, two exercise their full exit under the original put, and one, John's friend, Bert, who had invested alongside Jeffrey's group, chooses not to exercise either—retaining his full equity position. John swears to himself that, someday, that will prove to have been the wisest choice.

CHAPTER 10

It is May, 2015, making it eleven years since Victech was founded and three and a half years since they dodged the put option threat held by Jeffrey and the original investors. John taps his glass to get the attention of the attendees at the celebratory dinner for the company closing its first Venture Capital funding round.

The Refectory, a restaurant, is a long-standing Columbus favorite. The venue has a storied history as a church, a schoolhouse, and eventually, an upscale French restaurant. Seated around the elegant, private dining room are CEO John and Lynn Victor, Lead V.C. investor Carl Redder of RashCap Ventures and his wife Ramona, V.C.

investor Ed Duple with his wife Trudy, V.C investor Richard Greene of Domore Capital, John's friend and Board director, Katy Curtis, with her husband Jacques, and Victech CFO Marianne Higgins. The formal cocktail hour had turned into cocktail hours, interwoven with the Refectory's impeccable multi-course meals. The wine is now flowing, and the spirited group is getting louder.

John taps his glass once again, successfully quieting the group before leading off the toasts.

"We want to offer our sincere thanks and congratulations to our new investors and Board members. Carl, Katy, Dick, and Ed: we welcome you to the Victech family. Here is to many great and successful years of partnership."

Cheers are heard all around the tables.

Carl stands and raises his glass. He is stockily built with a booming voice and forceful presence.

"Thank you, John. You have built a great team here, and we look forward to growing Victech into a world-class powerhouse. As you may be aware, I have done this before—I know what it takes to build this company into a unicorn. It requires speed and unmatched aggressiveness. This company will dominate. It will plow through the obstacles that cause weaker players to stumble. Ed, Katy, and Dick: I look forward to working with you on our new Board as we show John's team how to become unstoppable."

Marianne glances quickly to John, who shrugs at her. OK, sounds a tad over the top, but perhaps that's his style. Probably wine-fueled too.

Carl sits back down and Katy stands, signaling she is next.

"I have known John for many years, both as a friend and as someone who has shared with me the countless joys and tribulations of bootstrapping a company. I am so happy John and his team have now reached this stage, and I'm thrilled to join his Board. I look forward to working with this fine assembled group."

As more toasts follow Katy's, Lynn scans the room trying to learn the cast of characters. Unlike John, her own career has never been her guiding star. While she enjoys her part-time job as a travel agent working out of home, it will always take a back seat to family. In addition to being the affable spouse of the CEO, her self-appointed role tonight is to ascertain who in this room could be a threat to her husband, his company, and therefore, her family.

John would tell her she was crazy if she were to share her private agenda, but for all his intelligence, Lynn knows her husband can be incredibly naïve. Lucky for him, her protective instincts are fully deployed for the mission at hand.

Sitting to Lynn's immediate right is Carl's wife, Ramona, an attractive woman wearing a business-like black pants suit and white blouse. Lynn estimates her age to be early forties. She has dark, black hair and neatly cut bangs. John had told Lynn that Carl's wife is a high-powered corporate consultant. Carl's toast makes Lynn wonder how a marriage can survive both parties having all-consuming jobs like theirs.

"Ramona, John tells me you are a consultant. What sort of clients do you work with?" Lynn asks.

"All sorts of enterprises, really. I must say—I adore this restaurant. Do you know its history? I understand it was once a church."

"I know, it's amazing. We don't dine here very often between John's million-hour work weeks and my own schedule. I work from home for a travel company. It's part time, though. My full-time job these days seems to be as a chauffeur for our daughter. Do you have kids?"

"We do not. I wonder which sections of this building are original. I suspect the floor above us housed the pews."

Lynn is thinking, Gee, thanks for sharing the personal info. Nice chatting with you so openly. It's like talking to a wall.

Lynn next attempts to strike up conversation with Ed's wife, Trudy, seated on her left. Remarkably, Trudy proves even less forthcoming than Ramona. Maybe she is just introverted. While Trudy silently swills her wine, Lynn tries to compensate for the communication deficit by talking openly about the challenges of raising an eight-year-old. Unrequited conversation soon makes it apparent that Ed's wife simply does not want to be at this affair.

***

In the car ride home, Lynn and John share observations. Lynn explains she had found Ramona to be secretive and not terribly social.

"I could not pry anything out of her. Her life, her work, her family. It was all 'What a stylish and historic restaurant' and other superficial blather."

"Hmm. Not surprised she didn't talk shop. She works

for Interthon Group, the global consultancy. Massive company. They are sort of like therapists for businesses. Confidentiality is coin of the realm in that world."

"Still, it felt like she was dodging me. No idea why. And who is that younger V.C.? Is he married?"

"Dick Greene. I think he may be engaged. Don't really know him yet. Seems to be a freshly minted MBA which is a red flag to me." Lynn looks puzzled. John says: "Suggests no real-world experience."

"I get it. And what did you think of Carl's toast? I thought it was weirdly hyperbolic."

"Yes, even bellicose!" John laughs. His hope is that Carl's installation as Board Chair will prove a major win for Victech. Carl Redder brings to the table unmatched bona fides, including early investment in two Silicon Valley unicorns, a term used as shorthand for privately held companies, valued at one billion dollars or more. Since transplanting himself and Ramona to Columbus, he has also raised one of the largest funds in the Midwest for his firm, RashCap Ventures. Even so, John is not preoccupied by the assertiveness of Carl's toast.

"And what about Ed's wife, Trudy? For whatever reason, she didn't want to be there tonight."

"I don't know him well yet, and I just met her tonight. He's friendly and also a numbers geek. Seems like a good sort."

"I think their marriage is in trouble."

"Really? You think those two are MOT?"

Lynn processes for a moment, wondering what that could stand for. "Ah. Matter of time."

John nods.

"Nice collection of Stepford wives you've assembled here, dear."

"Hold on. How about Katy?" John and Lynn have known her since before their daughter was born. "Do I get credit for bringing her onto the Board?"

"Yes, you get brownie points for landing her. She's super well respected in this town, especially as a role model for female entrepreneurs." Lynn can't resist adding, "So, I guess you figure one out of four ain't bad?"

John shakes his head. "I think I'm four for four. We'll just have to agree to disagree."

"Sorry, I can't go along with that."

"So, you disagree to disagree?"

"Not buying that either."

CHAPTER 11

It is January, 2016. Henry Li enters Lyra's office. Hired less than a year earlier, Henry knows Lyra considers him to be her best wordsmith. He has unofficially become the marketing "voice" of Victech." At this moment, however, Henry dreads being the bearer of bad news. He waves the single sheet draft brochure. "I could have gone all day without seeing this. I would love to un-see it."

"A real retina-burner, huh? I hate when that happens." Lyra's hand is outstretched. "Let's have a look." She peruses the page rapidly, muttering under her breath.

"It's a dead-on copy," Henry offers. "Typical Carbonara bullshit."

Just hearing Henry speak that name gives Lyra a headache. Carbonara is a knock-off competitor who appeared out of nowhere a few years back. Early on, friendly Victech customers and sales prospects had given Victech a heads-up that some company was claiming their new product had the same functionality as Victech's product but at a steeply reduced price. Recently, Carbonara announced a similar suite of products solidifying its reputation for exorbitant claims and dirty tricks.

But this is different.

This is the first piece of hard evidence that Carbonara has somehow acquired information on the most closely-guarded Victech internal project, called Sage, which is still under active development.

Henry watches Lyra process this information. As always, he is struck by her diverse skill set; the fact that she is both analytically astute and highly creative is a rare combination, but she is also wickedly funny and physically attractive. While Henry will not let his mind wander there for long, he enjoys her company and reminds himself how fortunate he is to have her as his boss.

She looks up from the page, grimacing.

"Not a good start to a new year. You know where their

name comes from, Henry? Sounds like an Italian dish, doesn't it? Don't be fooled. Long ago, there was something called carbon paper that made really shitty copies of original documents. That was apparently their role model." Henry laughs and Lyra sighs. "Well, we know what we're up against. We need to inform John and Sales."

CHAPTER 12

The V.C. funding brings a new seven-person Board of Directors. The insiders are John and CFO Marianne Higgins. Joining them is Company Counsel Tim Weatherly. The three institutional investors are Chairman Carl Redder, Ed Duple, and Dick Greene. The seventh member is Katy Curtis. While not an institutional investor, Katy made a modest sidecar investment in the V.C. funding round. As a concession made during funding negotiations, she would be considered a full voting member alongside the other V.C. directors. While not strictly an insider, John liked the idea of having a friend among the new Board members.

Board meetings are held quarterly, usually within ten days of the end of the prior quarter. The timing barely gives Marianne's finance team time to assemble the requisite reports needed for the meeting, and subsequent adjustments are often required as a result of the time crunch. As CFO, Marianne has repeatedly requested more time be allowed to assure the revenue and expense numbers have sufficiently gelled. Could we at least allow a minimum of two weeks to prepare? She had asked John.

Today, for the second time, he presents this as a formal motion only to be shot down by Carl, who quickly dismisses the request.

"We are a fast-growing company and cannot deal in obsolete statistics. Perhaps Marianne's team needs to get its act together."

He's speaking to the group as if Marianne is not sitting there, which is pure Carl, thinks John. He seems to choose the most abrasive approach possible for any given moment. He has Silicon Valley arrogance but lacks basic Midwestern amiability, John concludes but then wonders if his own assessment is too narrow-minded. It's one thing to have a bias for action, but why be so confrontational? Aren't we all on the same team?

Ed offers a suggestion: "Marianne, I would be happy to sit down with you and discuss possible ways we could optimize quarterly reporting procedures."

If Carl had made the same suggestion, it would have sounded condescending and compounded his prior insult. But Ed Duple runs an outside accounting practice specializing in small businesses. Furthermore, he is Mister Non-Confrontational—very even keel. It is clearly a genuine offer to assist.

"Thanks, Ed. Let's talk offline," Marianne responds.

John proceeds to work the agenda. He presents the results for the prior quarter, including color commentary on sales opportunities and projections. There is less discussion than usual, likely because the Directors are awaiting the report on the elephant in the room, of which John has already given them a heads-up notice.

John soon initiates the awaited topic. "As you all are aware, our upcoming release, scheduled to be announced next month, will mark the grand unveiling of Project Sage." It was customary to use only internal code names when referencing secret projects, both in verbal and written discussion. Project Sage refers to new product extensions that strengthen the Victech product line by using AI technology. It represents a big bet on the company's future growth path. "Last month, we heard rumors that Carbonara would be making some sort of announcement this week. A couple of days ago, we were able to capture a draft of it from one of our friendly customers which Carbonara is trying to unhook from us. I am sorry to report that it appears to be a dead ringer for Project Sage."

There is a brief silence, followed by a flurry of muttering from around the table, before Katy asks the question on everyone's mind.

"Could this be a coincidence?"

John shakes his head. "I can't see it being a coincidence. It's just too damn close."

Marianne elaborates, "It matches Sage feature by feature. It could have been drafted by us. Come to think of it, it was."

"Who leaked it?" demands Carl.

John shakes his head. "No idea."

"Can we accelerate our release?" Ed asks John.

"Too risky. We are in first stages of QA testing. We have early adopters lined up, but it is premature for Beta testing. Current test phase is really Alpha."

Sighs and groans fill the room.

Carl suddenly asserts, "Time for polygraphs."

"You want us to administer lie detector tests? To whom?" John blinks in disbelief.

"Everyone with knowledge of Sage," Carl says without hesitating.

Dick nods, "I agree—it will send the right message."

Are they fucking serious? John tries to contain his anger. "We have a worn-down tech team working around the clock and busting their asses for months. They have just now learned the competition is poised to leap-frog us, and you guys are proposing our message to the team is that we suspect they're traitors?"

Carl remains adamant. "You have a mole in your organization. Any competent CEO would want to do whatever is needed to find out where the leak is."

"I don't agree, Carl," Tim interjects. "You risk demoralizing the staff. That could be very damaging."

Everyone can feel the tension in the room rising, so Katy intervenes to get them back on track before it escalates.

"John, what is your recommendation?"

John regains his composure and responds thoughtfully. "I'm willing to bet on our team. Sage will be a much deeper, better built, and more thorough solution. We will be the long-term winner. Let Carbonara precede us by a few days on the announcement. We can accelerate our own announcement somewhat but hold fast to our delivery timetable. Alerting our customers and prospects about the upcoming Victech capabilities will give them pause. They will not suddenly jump ship to Carbonara. Sage will have a long lifespan. We have to approach this as a marathon, not a sprint."

CHAPTER 13

With the spread of the pandemic beginning in early March of 2020—the sales cycle became even more protracted. Victech transitioned quickly to a work-at-home model with most company meetings conducted via Slack, Zoom, and other online tools. As a software company with no manufacturing component, one might imagine Victech ideally positioned to weather the business shut-downs of 2020-2021. However, many Victech customers are hospitals, insurers, and other health care facilities. Throughout this period, these organizations were being buffeted by numerous challenges, including issues of capacity, worker shortages, vaccine availability, and changing government mandates. Consequently, only the largest organizations were making new tech investments of the scope Victech was seeking.

It has been over five years since the Victech AI solution, formerly Project Sage, was introduced. Since then, it has become the centerpiece of most new Victech sales, increasing the revenue from an average sale dramatically. The pandemic has narrowed the target market and increased the length of the sales cycle, so even though the higher price point creates greater revenue surges, it is only from very large organizations. At the same time, Carbonara continues to refine their own AI solution, and although it is repeatedly shown to be an inferior product, they continue to nibble away at the market and slow the decision-making process, as prospects are required to evaluate both products as part of their due diligence.

It is now mid-September, 2021, and the Sales Reps have been missing their target numbers across the board. Walt Masters, Victech's Sales Director for the past year, is presenting his turnaround strategy on a Zoom call with members of the senior staff.

"We need to recognize today's market for what it is," Walt explains. "HCOs are simply not looking to make six or seven figure investments in this environment. We need to regroup in our approach to these big AI enterprise sales by breaking them down into bite-size pieces. I believe we need to begin selling some base modules as starters that will put them on an upgrade path over time. In other words, focus on fast dimes instead of slow quarters."

Lyra interjects, "I completely disagree with that strategy, Walt. That will result in slow dimes. Breaking down the functionality would damage our holistic value proposition. It cannot be linearly dismantled, and attempting to do so would devalue the product and hurt our market image. You currently have large sales moving slowly. Your proposed approach would transform that into many tiny sales stalling out entirely."

Walt pushes on, overlooking her main point. "We need to get the price point down, Lyra."

"I don't think so. Our problem is not a pricing objection. Product value is demonstrable. Look at Aerie."

Aerie Health Insurance was among the biggest customer wins for Victech. From the start, this national giant has continued to gobble up smaller insurers on an almost monthly basis. Each merger requires Aerie to expand their investment in Victech to manage their claims.

Walt is flustered. "They are the exception to the rule. How many Aeries do you think are out there?"

"There are enough. And each one we sell creates more as we build demand downstream. The productivity boost we deliver to large HCOs is gaining recognition as a state-of-the-art industry standard. They are becoming an aspiration for smaller organizations. But selling it ala carte would be destructive to the perceived value."

John heads off this discussion before Walt digs in and it devolves into a one-on-one debate.

"Walt, I understand what you're saying, and we all share your frustration about our protracted selling cycle. But that's the point. We need a strategy focused on how to build urgency and accelerate the buying process. Perhaps that means a different approach in how we sell into large organizations. We could even offer additional payment flexibility or make some other minor concessions, but I agree with Lyra, deconstructing the product is not the right approach."

Walt swallows his frustration and does not persist. "Alright. Let me work with those comments and circle back to the group."

When the Zoom call ends, John privately contacts Lyra

using Slack audio.

"OK, now tell me what you were not saying to Walt."

Lyra is primed for the question. "We should be riding out this slowdown by focusing one-hundred-percent on bagging elephants. Our value is optimal for the larger enterprises, and they help us grow our reputation more rapidly. They also provide us the best margin by far. Additionally, they are the only things still slogging along in this languorous economy."

"They're slower than hell to close."

"True, but that's not solely due to their innate bureaucracy. We are using the wrong tool for the job."

"You're referring to Walt?"

"Not just Walt, John. It's our whole Sales team. With maybe a couple exceptions, we do not have a team of high-end closers. These large enterprise sales require multiple touch points to assure individual departments are being brought along throughout the sale process. Otherwise, we risk being surprised when someone in IT, or just out of nowhere, impedes or vetoes the purchase. The ideal sales model calls for a Senior Account Director orchestrating the process with additional team members reporting to that person. The team needs to work and monitor each department of the enterprise that could become a veto threat."

It is clear to John that something has to change, and much of Lyra's analysis rings true for him. It mirrors and advances his own current thinking on how to turn things around. What she is suggesting, however, will require great agility by Victech and entail major disruption to the business. John wonders if his Victech ship can alter course that swiftly.

"You know this sounds expensive as hell," he said.

"Yes, terribly. Unless… we close even a single giant, in which case it will pay for itself many times over. This is where we are. This is what it takes for us to ride out this slump and get to the next level."

John asks Lyra to document how she would configure the ideal Sales team based on her vision. This includes identifying which members of the current team are qualified to be one of the Account Directors of record and those who would be more effective in working on enterprise accounts under the A.D.

If this concept is to become their new strategy, they will need to move very fast.

CHAPTER 14

John receives an email from Dick Greene requesting a one-on-one Zoom call. The agenda is ostensibly to discuss Victech's headcount. John is slightly surprised by the request since Dick rarely takes initiative as a Board director, usually content to just serve as a shadow for Carl.

John accepts the invitation, and Dick's face soon appears on the screen.

"Hi, John. Thanks for jumping on this call last minute. In the last Board meeting, you walked through the members of your senior staff, explaining their roles in the company. I want to discuss your H.R. Director, in particular."

"Sure. That would be Marcus. He has been with us for almost ten years. What about him?"

"I want to ask you if you believe a senior staff position is appropriate for an individual in a Human Resources role?"

"Absolutely. Why do you ask?"

"First, know that this isn't about Marcus personally—it's about the H.R. position."

Where the hell is this discussion going? John is thinking. It's definitely off to a bad start.

Before giving John a chance to comment, Dick continues, "In successful business models, senior staff slots are reserved for the more important roles like Sales, Development, Marketing, and Finance. For my firm's portfolio companies, we consider H.R. superfluous to operations."

"I strongly disagree, Dick. For any company with more than a couple dozen employees, having a solid H.R. department with a strong leader is essential."

"But John, these days, there are numerous H.R. outsource services covering everything from benefits management to mentoring automation. It simply isn't a needed position—especially at the salary level of your H.R.

Director."

It occurs to John that Dick truly has no clue as to how tech companies operate, so he attempts to explain. "One key role of H.R. is to keep the CEO informed of what is happening within the team, especially as it grows in size. A skilled H.R. executive can anticipate and prevent numerous issues within the team. They can provide an outlet for growing frustrations, grievances, and personnel disputes before they become serious. They earn the trust of the managers. They are often the go-to individual for problems that some team members would not be comfortable taking directly to the CEO. Since last year, we have had to navigate a transition to a hybrid home-remote working model to dodge COVID. H.R. played an essential role in that transition; communicating with the team, smoothing the changes, and retaining loyalty."

Over the Zoom call, Dick stares at John as if he just arrived from Mars. He is startled by John's description of what he considers an unpublished role of H.R. In Dick's textbook experience, startup business models do not call for a psychologist, a social worker, or whatever the hell it is that John just described.

Ignoring Dick's apparent bafflement, John continues.

"In our particular case, Marcus is amiable, smart, and intuitive. He is close to all of our critical workers which are the beating heart of the organization. He keeps us between the ditches. He screens new applicants and assesses their compatibility. I think of him as one of the load-bearing walls of Victech."

"Okay, John. I will take what you've said under advisement." Dick is still dumbfounded and ends the call with John soon after.

John reflects on the call with amazement. Is this what MBA programs are teaching these days? That H.R. executives are dead weight? Do they even understand that startup companies are comprised of real people? MBAs have apparently concluded that success is formulaic. The ignorance is stunning and troubling. John quietly notes that this could become another unwelcomed and destabilizing challenge for him during this turbulent time.

CHAPTER 15

In November of 2021, Lyra is promoted to V.P. of Sales and Marketing, with Henry Li backfilling her prior role as Marketing Director. In her expanded role, she quickly sets about restructuring and upgrading the Sales team. The former Sales Director, Walt, had kindly resigned before being asked to do so. The three most senior Sales Reps became Account Directors, each having several Account Representatives whose revised mission is to provide blanket coverage for high-end enterprise accounts. Marcus helps John and Lyra revise sales compensation plans, while preparing new hire requisitions to stage the transition to a more upscale sales team.

Lyra also initiates formation of an Advisory Board, consisting of a dozen top Victech customers, all of whom agree to meet in person as a group two to three times a year to discuss new tech requirements that Victech can potentially address. These exclusive meetings provide key customers an opportunity to influence product direction based upon their needs. They prove mutually beneficial as the meetings also become Victech's most valuable source for optimizing the company's product roadmap.

***

It is now April, 2022. Despite the progress, the Company once again finds itself in a financial squeeze. It is the unwelcome return of John's Second Lesson of Startups: Success Burns Through Money Faster.

For this reason, John has assembled the Senior Staff and asked Marianne to share the company's financial status. Marianne walks through the numbers and offers her own summary to the group. "It should be obvious we are in trouble. Our cashflow from new and recurring sales is inadequate, and our burn rate has grown substantially from new hiring, including generous, nonrecoverable draws for sales hires. We have become overly reliant on a small number of very large customers."

Lyra responds forcefully but without anger, addressing the group. "But wasn't this the plan? To hire a top-end sales team with an emphasis on bagging elephants? That is exactly what we are doing. And it is working. Look at Aerie. They are delivering seven figures of revenue for us every quarter. Isn't this what we have V.C.s for? Can we get old Carl to cough up some cash?"

Marianne looks to John to explain, so he jumps in. "Our VC investors signed up for a five-year ride, seven years ago. They wanted an exit in 2020, and we persuaded them to allow two more years due to COVID. They have made it clear they are tired and resistant to investing more."

Lyra doesn't want to hear it. "It takes six to nine months to get sales productivity from new hires at this level. We offer nonrecoverable draws to preserve their earnings because that's what it takes to attract this caliber of talent. Look at the pipeline. It is working."

Henry, now Marketing Director, asks, "John, I don't understand how anyone could possibly plan how long it will take for a company to have an exit? It's unknowable.

It can take years, if it ever even happens."

"You are correct, Henry," John replies. "It can be two or twenty years. Longer even. It is one of many odd conceits that investors believe they can dictate timetables for startups to succeed. Many investors say they like to buy into startups at an early stage—but most companies haven't even identified their sweet spot during their early years. Slack thought it was producing an online game, but wound up selling the tool they had developed for internal use to optimize their email. X, once known as Twitter was established as a utility using SMS to exchange small, inconsequential messages within a group. Artificial and arbitrary goals established by institutional investors can inhibit essential serendipity from occurring. But startups fail when they run out of money, which means when the investors become impatient."

"Can we get additional investors?" Henry asks.

Marianne again looks to John, who nods, giving her permission to disclose the other issue. "As part of the 2015 funding terms, our V.C.'s accrue dividends on their investment each month. Well, those dividends have compounded for the past seven years and..." her voice falters.

"We don't have the money to pay them off," Lyra finishes the sentence. "And that accrued debt is enough to scare off any new investors, right?"

"Boy, are you fast." John flashes a smile at Lyra and turns to Marianne. "You don't want to play the hand slap game with Lyra." He addresses the group, "Listen, it's OK. Don't panic. As senior staff, we want you all to know where we are. We are evaluating possible solutions and we have months to come up with something. In the meantime, everybody needs to keep pushing. We've escaped from worse jams than this before, and we'll do it again."

John adjourns the meeting. He successfully anticipates the two-word Slack message he will receive from Marianne. "Will we?"

CHAPTER 16

As the Company's precarious financial situation weighs on him during the day, John looks to his home life for a brief respite from the stress. This compartmentalization technique has been a reliable tactic of his for years. Time with his family, a good dinner, some wine, and music usually do the trick. He relies on the temporary escape to enable him to charge back into the fray, fully recharged for tomorrow's fire drills.

However, such relaxation is not within reach today. Lynn calls him as he is leaving the office and tells him they need to talk tonight. Her tone strikes an ominous chord.

He braces himself for what is to come.

As he enters through the front door, Lynn pounces. "I'm sorry, but this has been on my mind for some time," she begins. "It's about Maddy."

John follows Lynn into the kitchen, where they both take a seat at the table. She tells John that Maddy has seemingly transitioned from an active, loving child who adored her parents into a glum, nontalkative fifteen-year-old overnight.

Has John noticed? No, of course not.

Lynn is clearly distraught. "I don't know what has happened to her in the last few months. It's like she's a whole other person."

"Isn't that why they call it the terrible teens?"

"No. That's not it. It's like she's undergoing some sort of trauma which she won't talk about."

"Oh, come on. What sort of problems can a smart and popular fifteen-year-old girl possibly have?"

This sets Lynn off.

"Were you born yesterday? You aren't that stupid, John. Where should I begin? Let's see, boys, appearance, school pressure, menstruation, drugs, social life, online media, bullying, dating, friendships. Shall I go on?"

"Please, don't. I get your point. How are her friends?"

"Remember Fredrick? He took her to that school dance last spring and became her first boyfriend, sort of—she was on cloud nine that night. But that's suddenly gone. I don't think she's seen him in months. No idea what happened there. She spends all her time with Susan, her BFF. There were a couple circles of friends the two of them used to hang with sometimes, but again, not anymore." Lynn sighs, then continues wistfully, "Both girls used to be so energetic, so positive. Lately, they both walk around with this heavy hangdog look. I cannot get Maddy to talk about it. Is despondency some known teen phase? Is that a thing? If I push her to talk about it, she just glares at me. It's getting worse." She pauses before adding: "You might be aware of what is happening in your own family, John, if you were home more often."

There it is. Lynn is no longer willing to repress her feelings on this topic. Those long-ago concerns about income were assuaged when the V.C.s entered the picture, and John began to draw an appropriate salary. But the many demands of the company have, once again, made twelve-hour work days the norm. Even as the company's growth accelerates, Victech seems to face a witch's brew of threats, including a financial squeeze, investor pressures, competitive intelligence leaks, and personnel issues.

"I'm doing the best I can, babe," John says. "I'll talk to Maddy and try to get her to open up."

Lynn just looks down, shaking her head.

They both sit in silence for a few minutes before he asks, "You OK?"

"Yeah. Sometimes, I just miss my eight-year-old daughter, though."

CHAPTER 17

As Victech's longtime H.R. Director, Marcus' role in interviewing prospective employees has grown beyond the limited and rote functions of answering questions about Victech, its policies, benefits, etc. Despite Dick's suggestion to John last year that the executive level H.R. position is superfluous, Marcus is increasingly recognized as a shrewd judge of character, and hiring managers have come to appreciate the unique insights he is able to glean. The candidate he met with today, who was seeking a Customer Service position, required extra scrutiny since her current employer is Carbonara—Victech's main competitor. Marcus forewarns the hiring manager to be extremely careful during their meetings with her, and to not divulge any non-public information or unfairly grill the candidate on things she is not at liberty to discuss.

Marcus sits in Lyra's office debriefing her on the interviews.

"Did we play nice with her, Marcus?" Lyra asks.

"I think so. Although, I did not participate in her meeting with the hiring manager. He tends to lack boundaries sometimes."

"You think?" she laughs. "Is this candidate any good?"

"The hiring manager is unimpressed. And honestly speaking, I got the impression she is just sniffing around."

"Do you mean competitively, for her current employer? Or just tire-kicking whether she wants a career change?"

"I can't be entirely certain. When I asked her why she wants to consider a new job, she complained that her present company is run by outside consultants. She made it sound like a very flat org structure. The implication seems to be a lack of upward mobility."

They discuss the candidate for a few more minutes, both readily agreeing she is not a good fit. Marcus takes the opportunity to ask Lyra a question that has been on the top of his mind for days. "The last senior staff meeting haunts me, Lyra. It sounds like our investors don't want to support us any longer, and we cannot raise new funds due to the debt. Banks won't touch us, so what other sources of funding are there? What happens if we run dry?"

Lyra responds warmly, "No answers yet, but please know John works best in the clutch." She can tell Marcus does not find reassurance in this statement. "That may not sound like much, but from my experience, you can take great solace in that. I've seen him pull us out of worse."

CHAPTER 18

The girl smelled the alcohol as soon as she entered her house. Maybe I'll get lucky and find him passed out, she thought, although it seemed unlikely at 6:00 p.m. As she walks toward the kitchen, the unruly man suddenly appears at the top of the stairs, holding an empty glass.

"Da fuck? You sneak in?" he demands.

Nice to see you too. "I just got home."

"School let out hours ago. Da hell you been?"

Walking around the neighborhood, hoping wouldn't be conscious when I got home. "I was with Maddy. We're working on a school project…"

He has lost interest in her reply. Ignoring the girl, he staggers down the stairs, heading toward the kitchen. Seeing that he's wearing a stained undershirt and boxers, she is disgusted by him and refuses to look at his large, hairy body. The man finds his bottle of Jack Daniels on the counter and tops off his glass. "Your mom's pulling second shift tonight. Mac & cheese on the stove, if you want."

"Not hungry," she replies. "I'm going to lay down."

She climbs the stairs to her room, locks the door, and flops on the bed. Her mother will be gone until at least midnight. She does not like being alone in the house with him. I need to get out of here, she thinks. This is unbearable. He needs to go away and leave both of us alone. Mother is weak and afraid to challenge him. She pretends she doesn't know what he does to me. She brought him into our house—this is her fault. She has deserted me. Alone with her thoughts, the girl grows more resentful of her mother.

She is startled by a sudden, loud banging on the bedroom door. The man is yelling while pounding the door with his fist. "Whad I tell you about locking doors?"

"I just want to sleep, Kyle. Please, go away."

"I'll break this fucking door down, Susie. Swear. Then

you 'splain to your ma why it's broke." He starts kicking the door violently.

"Stop!" she screams, running to unlock the door before it breaks.

He bursts into the room, shoving her hard onto the bed. In the process, the man stumbles on top of her, pinning her down. Coughing and slurring his words, he says, "Susie, you is so bad."

The girl squirms to break free. He is a large man, who stinks of sweat and booze. She starts to gag. His chest is crushing her, and she's having trouble taking full breaths. He shifts slightly, and she catches her breath while still pinned to the bed. "Please. I won't lock the door anymore, I promise." She feels his fat hand on her leg under her skirt. "Please, don't."

As the encroachment progresses, the girl thinks of other things. Anything but this. Once again, she must divert her mind to escape her body's suffering. She is no longer here in this room. She is with Maddy—they are dancing and joking about stupid TikTok videos they have shared. Laughing at the new, younger kids in their school. Now she and Maddy are trying on clothes in Aeropostale and rating the boys in their class. The girl has detached from her body.

She is mercifully unaware of the tears streaming down her own face. In her mind, she visits a happier time and place.

CHAPTER 19

The outside tables on the Polaris Grill patio are generously spaced, making it a good place for private meetings. The tall, middle-aged African American man sports an OSU cap which covers most of the gray. He sits in one corner, nursing his coffee, as John approaches.

"Danny, great to see you again."

"Hi, John. Always good to see my fellow barfly."

They hug as John laughs and says, "That's been a while."

John has known Danny Thurmond since 2003. They first became acquaintances while working out at the same gym. One day, Danny asked John to join him for drinks that weekend, which began a long-standing weekly ritual of dining, bar-hopping, and scouting for girls. At ages twenty-seven and thirty, John and Danny were both in the formative stages of their careers. John was a tech manager at Aurelian, and Danny was a rookie in the Columbus police force. The bar scene actually produced a rare win for Danny when he met Allie, who would become his future wife. It was the same year John was introduced to Lynn through a common acquaintance. Both men married their respective sweethearts the following year.

Danny retired from the police force two years ago to start his new career as a private detective. As one of his first cases, John hired him to help retrieve company property from a former remote employee who had decided to keep it after he was fired for incompetence. All told, the tech gear he stole wasn't especially valuable, but the former employee had given John his word he would ship back the equipment promptly. Instead, the gentleman relocated himself one night, taking care not to leave any forwarding address. Danny's approach was to set a trap which would cause the thief to reveal his location. He sent a fake email offering cash for used tech gear, which lured the former employee to park his car at a designated building. When he walked away to a nearby alley, as directed by the email, Danny was able to plant a GPS tracking device under the rear of the man's car. This tactic allowed Danny to follow the car, learn the man's new address, and recover the stolen property along with police backup. John was impressed both with the cleverness of Danny's plan and the quick results.

As they finish ordering lunch, John describes the problem of the Company's leaked product plans.

Danny is always a quick study. He listens and pays close attention before he weighs in. "So, you have a mole, eh? How many people in your company knew about the new release?"

"Almost everyone. We try to keep the troops informed."

"I would say that is at least one too many."

John smiles and nods. "Brilliant. Where do we go from here?"

"How long has this been going on?"

"On and off for a few years. Sometimes, it seems like coincidence when Carbonara announces a new feature, since their basic product line is modeled so closely after ours. But they copied our big move into AI almost word for word. There's no way it wasn't leaked."

"Do your folks have non-compete agreements?"

"Sure, but these days, you know they are more of a non-disclosure with heavy focus on confidentiality."

"Understood. I wouldn't expect a lockup agreement from you, John. Locking folks out of their chosen field is out of vogue," Danny says, laughing.

"It was never in vogue for me," John says.

Lunch is soon served. The two of them brainstorm over sandwiches and salads. After much discussion, Danny outlines a tentative plan to find the mole.

By the time John returns to his car, he feels reassured he is retaining the best person for the job and looks forward to working with Danny again.

CHAPTER 20

When Lyra was first promoted to V.P. of Sales and Marketing, some backroom chatter attributed her rapid rise to cleavage and tight skirts. But the snark did not persist long. Her credibility and wit were reaffirmed in each contact she made and every time she spoke. Her natural interpersonal skills and intelligence quickly made fans and allies. Any naysayers who remained kept grudges to themselves. It is also known that as a member of the Senior Staff, she has John's complete confidence and is increasingly perceived as the number two executive in the company.

Lyra and John would often lunch together to get away

from the office, especially for private deliberations. Today, it is a late lunch at Hunan Lion where they discuss sales prospects over wonton soup and orange shrimp. Lyra wants to talk further about cash flow and the investor situation when John abruptly changes the direction of conversation.

"New topic, Lyra. I want to discuss a fresh company direction, and I need your help in planning it."

"All ears."

"It involves Victech moving into VR."

There is a brief silence before Lyra laughs out loud. Really? Virtual Reality had become a standing joke within the company. A staggering number of investments made by multiple companies in this technology had either ended badly or, worse yet, failed to end at all. At this time, it has become the Tech industry's largest multi-car pileup. Although, the market has yet to render a final verdict, deep-pocket tech companies have been repeatedly burned attempting to find the right problem to justify a VR solution.

She looks at John for signs of satire. Nothing. "Wait. You're being serious?"

He nods. "It's OK. Shoot from the hip."

Where to begin?

"Should we discuss the countless field failures of this technology, including the Army's use of wearable goggles? We cannot afford the sort of bet-the-company gamble Microsoft or Meta is taking. Our customers are not gamers. What is the augmented reality application for health insurers? What is the play with simulated aromas? How about those vests with sensations? Other haptics? You've said as much yourself; I don't know of any VR application that makes sense for our market…"

She catches herself and pauses before her response turns into a rant. Is he testing me? she wonders. She studies his face again; no clues.

Regrouping, she calmly suggests: "OK, I can pull together a skunk works from Dev and Sales to brainstorm this topic. Some of our best blue-sky nerds," she says, adding, "Once they stop laughing, that is."

"No. I'm just looking for a brochure draft. A marketing piece. I don't want anyone else in the loop at this stage. Just you. Think of it as a trial balloon. Speculate on the potential benefits."

This is weird as hell. Try not to show exasperation: "At a minimum, I'll need Henry to help construct this fiction.

He is discreet."

"That's fine. But make sure he gets it—no discussion with anyone else inside or outside the company."

"Done." Lyra returns to her food quietly. Her brain is racing.

Something is terribly wrong.

CHAPTER 21

Katy is calling John using a private Slack channel. He picks up immediately.

"Hi, John. This new product plan draft is confusing me. Virtual Reality?"

"It's an up-and-coming technology. The whole metaverse thing."

Ah yes, that up-and-comer that caused Meta's market value to plummet by $800 Billion. "In what way would our customers use it? I don't see the fit."

"Not many people saw the need for a personal computer on their desk in the mid-1970s. This is the next step in digitizing the human experience."

Silence.

Why is John resorting to buzzword blather? Katy is rarely rattled, but such a non-answer is out of character for him.

She presses on:. "This flyer you sent marked 'For Your Eyes Only.' Who has seen this besides me?"

"Just you, Ed, Dick, and Carl, for now. I want to keep the circle small."

"John, you should know that Carl is calling for the four of us to meet in executive session tomorrow to discuss the Company's financials. This VR product plan is inconsistent with the company's prior position. I fear it will be treated like a bombshell. It isn't going to help our situation."

John knows what she is saying. Carl wants to fire the CEO and dissolve the company if it cannot be monetized even at fire-sale prices. He has made it clear RashCap Ventures has had enough of Victech. He wants out and doesn't seem to care how messy the exit is.

There isn't anything else to say.

"I understand, Katy. Thanks for letting me know."

CHAPTER 22

Lyra places the limes on her kitchen counter and slices them into uniform wedges. She adds ice into both glasses before liberally adding Tito's vodka into each. Topping them off with a splash of tonic, she carries the drinks into the living room. Her guest is still standing while quietly jabbering away on his phone. His tone is clearly one of frustration. He takes the drink with his free hand while muttering something about "discussing this with your mother first" to the caller.

"Your daughter, I assume?" Lyra asks as he ends the call.

"Always. She takes advantage of the miserable

communications between Trudy and me these days. She plays us off one another."

"Can you blame her?" Lyra regrets saying it as soon as she sees his face.

"Sorry, I didn't mean to pile on, Eddie. But can you blame her for trying to make the best of a bad situation?"

"Enough," he says, raising two fingers. That is their symbol for invoking Rule #2, which calls for a change of subject.

Although neither of them ever used the word, the affair is now entering its sixth month with no signs of cooling. It began with a friendly chat between the two at Victech following a Board meeting, but from the start, she had found him to be adorably geeky. Their chat led to a lunch meeting, during which Lyra learned a lot more about this tall man who runs an accounting practice for small businesses. Very financially savvy, Ed sometimes invests alongside professional V.C.s as in the case of Victech. He also shared with her details of his personal life. With a son in college and a daughter starting her career in nursing, Ed Duple and his wife Trudy became empty nesters last year.

Their marriage started to crumble as the couple realized they no longer had much in common outside of their newly-adult children. They fought frequently abetted by Trudy's increased drinking and the fact that she had made it clear to him that she has no interest in his accounting practice or his investments. The man she had once regarded as a stable and reliable partner became an object of contempt, as she viewed him as a boring accountant with whom she was wasting her life.

Then Lyra entered his world.

From their first lunch together, Ed was infatuated with her. She seemed to have it all: brains, looks, sharp humor. That body. He had never been with such a woman or even assumed it was possible for someone like her to exist in the real world. Their rendezvous soon took the form of private dinner meetings. After their second one, Lyra invited him up to her apartment. They had a mutual agreement that discretion was always foremost. In addition to his failing marriage, Ed is a Director on the Board of the company, in which she is a top executive. There were many good reasons to maximize their secrecy. They would avoid any sort of interaction at the company and keep the appearance of being just business acquaintances.

As the months passed, their relationship grew its own personality beyond the trysts. Realizing the complexity of their situation, they developed a series of rules guiding their time alone together. These rules were a combination of Ed's list-oriented approach to all things, overlayed with Lyra's wicked sense of humor.

Rule #1: Err on the Side of Discretion. This is a general rule which applies to any situation that potentially raises the risk of their relationship being exposed.

Rule #2: Bluntly named Stay Out of My Shit. Under this rule, either party can halt any discussion they feel is too intrusive into their lives outside of their relationship. This also helps prevent inadvertent business disclosure breaches which might run afoul of Rule #1. Ed wanted to call this 'Stay in Your Lane,' but Lyra preferred the grittier SOS moniker.

Rule #3: Painful Honesty. A rule that creates commitment that each will remain truthful in disclosing their feelings for the other, regardless of the circumstances. Lyra says this can act like a circuit breaker to prevent her from becoming another Trudy. Ed says that could never happen, but he agrees it is a good rule.

At this moment, however, Rule #2 has been invoked, and Ed needs a break. Lyra quietly leaves the room. He is holding his drink, staring out of the window, and replaying the most recent altercation with Trudy in his mind. Her attacks have become vicious with neither forethought, nor filter, even criticizing him in public with deeply demeaning insults. The phone call with his daughter made it clear Trudy is trying to turn his daughter against him. It is no longer tolerable. This is not the same person Ed married twenty-three years ago. Tonight, perhaps for the first time, he accepts the reality that his marriage is truly over.

A gentle voice comes from behind, "Ahem."

Ed turns and looks at Lyra who has donned a new outfit for the occasion. She is wearing lingerie featuring a black, silk negligee. He whistles.

"Why Mistah Duple Sir, may I kindly request your presence in the boudoir?"

Ed laughs. "That may be the worst, most unintelligible accent I've ever heard. Some sort of southern belle?"

"Shut up. This is a seduction. You in or not?"

He approaches her admiringly. "Garter belt and all? I'm very impressed."

"Sure, all guys love this shit. It's gift wrapping. You can't wait to unwrap the package."

"Can I have more sexy voice, though, please? Just the vamp, no accent."

As breathily as she can muster, "Of course, Mr. Duple. You are absolutely correct, Mr. Duple. You are my guest here. How can I possibly make you more comfortable?"

They both laugh and clink glasses. "I can't tell if that is supposed to be Lauren Bacall or Marilyn Monroe. Do you do anyone still alive? Scarlett Johansson maybe?"

With the push of one finger, she coaxes him into a sitting position on the couch and climbs onto his lap. They kiss deeply. She slinks further into him and whispers in his ear, "Whatever you prefer tonight, Mr. Duple."

CHAPTER 23

Marianne has been despondent for months. Her heart is sullen and she cannot hide her morose countenance. As Victech's financial picture deteriorates, she had found that she no longer sleeps at night or functions well at the office. The CFO subtly offered her resignation to John the prior week. He refused to accept it and told her a solution was at hand. Solution? Not bloody likely, she thinks. Our burn rate is unsustainable, and thanks to the V.C. dividends coming due, we have a debt load that makes us ineligible for bank financing and unattractive to new investors.

"They're going to shut us down, John. I can't see an alternative," she had said.

"We're not dead yet," he replied. "Give me until Tuesday."

That was last Friday, and Marianne now enters John's office. He and Lyra are already at his conference table, happily chatting. God knows why, she thinks.

John motions for her to sit. "Good morning, Marianne. I'll cut right to the chase. What source of funding requires neither debt, nor equity?"

She raises an eyebrow. *A riddle? Are they asking me?*

"I've got nothing."

Lyra solves the puzzle, "Our customers are the source. At least our largest one may be. John recently asked me to approach Aerie Health about a multi-year license deal. They are in the process of acquiring other insurers at a blistering rate. Each merger expands our license footprint since they need us for claims processing across the enterprise. Therefore, we are essential to their expansion plans. We pitched them a seven-year all-you-can-eat agreement, fully paid up-front and steeply discounted. They were intrigued and have requested a term sheet detailing the transaction."

"All-you-can-eat?" asks Marianne.

"For the up-front charge, they can use our products for as many newly merged entities as they like for the next seven years. They will receive updates but must separately license any new products they might want which are developed over that period."

Marianne blinks. Her gears begin to turn. She is suddenly awake and fully engaged.

"That is incredible," she pauses but then asks, "But are we eating the seed corn?"

John responds: "That's a fair question. We are buying ourselves time, which is what we need most urgently."

The three discuss the next steps, in which Marianne will collaborate with Lyra, John, and company counsel to produce a term sheet that passes both financial and legal muster. John says it must be delivered to Aerie in the next two days.

That night, for the first time in many weeks, Marianne was surprised to find herself sleeping soundly through the entire night.

CHAPTER 24

Henry knocks on Lyra's office door. She waves him in as she finishes her phone call and notices Henry's look of bewilderment. Before she can say a word, Henry reads from his phone.

"Today, Carbonara Technologies announced its long-range plan to develop and incorporate advanced tools of Virtual Reality technology into its product line over the next twenty-four months," he stops reading and looks up at her. "We produced your top-secret flyer for John just last Friday. What the hell is this?"

Lyra absorbs the update, mulls it momentarily, and

smiles coyly. "Henry, I believe this is the sound of a trap springing."

***

Katy arrives at RashCap Ventures headquarters, approaches the security desk, and announces her visit to see Carl Redder. An escort leads her down the hall and into an enormous conference room where Ed, Dick, and Carl are already seated.

As coffee is served by a staffer, Carl begins recapping the discussion to her. John Victor is failing and should be removed as CEO. The original target for a liquidity exit for Victech was five years later but was later extended to seven. That period is now ending and there is no exit in sight. The Company is burning through cash and has no prospects for paying the accrued investor dividends. Over a year ago, the investors had forced John to try and sell the company, and he was unable to attract any takers. Despite the Company's growth, the intransigence of existing investors to re-up their investment, plus the Company's accrued debt, is more than enough to scare away new money.

Carl winds up his rant, "And now, we have this bizarre

Virtual Reality nonsense dropped on us. It makes no sense as a strategy. We can only conclude John is out of control and making reckless moves out of desperation."

Katy says, "I have an update on that. John called me last night. There is no VR plan. Apparently, there never was."

Carl is first to react, "What the hell?"

"He sent us a fictitious flyer? Why?" Ed asks.

"He says it was part of a plan to find out where the product leaks are coming from," Katy explains.

There is silence between the group, followed by incredulous looks around the table.

"This is outrageous!" Carl explodes. "He has deliberately lied to the Board and fed us false information. He must be removed for cause immediately."

Katy waves a slow-down hand and faces Carl: "The Company is making larger sales now and urgently needs fresh funding. You are the lead investor. Instead of supporting the business, you want us to cut off the oxygen and oust the CEO? Five minutes ago, your pretext for firing him was performance. Now, it's for cause. I, for one, would like us to sit down with John for a full and candid meeting and discuss all of these issues. Let's hear him out before any rash decision is made."

Carl will have none of it. "As Chairman, I am calling a vote on the immediate removal of John Victor as CEO of Victech Technologies. Discussion?"

"But who would replace him?" Dick asks. "Lyra is the next in line. Would she become the CEO?"

Carl responds, "Perhaps in the interim. We'll certainly want our own man at the helm long term, though."

Katy does not react to Carl's 'own man' reference. Instead, she continues with her original thought, "This is the wrong discussion. Removal of a CEO requires a lot of planning. Issues, including severance agreement and succession, need to be worked out. Company morale must be considered. It must not be done haphazardly. But I'm not even on that road, Carl, because I vote against John's termination."

"I support removing John as CEO," Dick says, ignoring Katy's objections.

Per the Investor's Rights Agreement, a majority of preferred investors is required for passage. All turn to Ed who appears ill-prepared to be the deciding vote.

"I am inclined to agree that John should be terminated based on what we know now," Ed begins thoughtfully, "but I also agree with Katy that he should have a chance to respond to these issues. So, I am not prepared to vote yet. I want us to meet with John before we pursue this vote."

After more discussion, Carl begrudgingly agrees they will meet with John and confront him with these concerns before making a final decision.

CHAPTER 25

As the organization has grown over the years, John's own one-on-one customer contact has diminished out of necessity. The reduced interaction is driven by having more customers and less personal CEO bandwidth. Notable exceptions include some of the company's first customers and also its largest. Both groups seem to believe they hold a permanent entitlement to have direct contact with the CEO of Victech.

It has been a couple of days since the multi-year Aerie proposal had been delivered. Lyra is on pins and needles awaiting their response, but it catches John off-guard when the call comes in for him, made personally from Steven

Saunders, CEO of Aerie.

"Steve, how are you?" John asks, hiding his surprise.

"Doing well, John, and glad that Victech apparently is also. Listen, I'll cut right to it. This multi-year proposal your team has assembled is attractive and well thought-out, although, we are going to have to decline. But I wanted to personally let you know we greatly respect the thinking and effort that went into it."

"What is the issue, Steve?"

"There are two key problems. Your proposal calls for the large purchase of an unbudgeted capital expense on short notice. More critically, the seven-year lifetime of the deal exceeds our near-term planning horizon. Make no mistake, your proposed discount structure is appealing and most appreciated. But over a time-span that long, there are just too many variables which substantially increase the risk."

"Understood," John says. The size of the proposed deal is large enough that John wonders if Steve has the authority to unilaterally approve it.

"If I may ask, did your Board reject it?"

"That's a fair question. Our next meeting occurs the week after next. I have not submitted it in advance knowing they would shoot it down for the same reasons I just described. Nor could I recommend it for approval myself for those reasons."

Not willing to give up, John takes another shot.

"Suppose it were a four-year deal, Steve?"

There is an unexpectedly long pause at the other end of the line before Steve asks: "Same discount structure?"

"Yes, and we can even stagger the payment due dates a bit."

Another brief pause. "Hmm. Have your folks write it up; we'll take another look."

"Thank you, Steve. We'll get on it."

"By the way, John, do it fast."

"You've got it."

CHAPTER 26

It is Monday evening when John receives Danny's text at 10:15 p.m. asking for them to meet the next morning at Starliner Diner, a favorite haunt in nearby Hilliard. What has he learned? John wants to text back, but he respects Danny's policy of not sharing content electronically. It isn't that Danny is old school. On the contrary, much of his work involves planting electronic bugs on people, places, and things. But even so, Danny fully understands the high risk of electronic communications being intercepted. So instead, John agrees but says it must be early since a Board meeting has been called for later that morning.

The next morning, John sits at the diner, waiting for

Danny to arrive. This time, it is John who is on his second cup of coffee when Danny finally joins him.

"What have we learned?" John asks, before Danny has even had a chance to sit down.

"Good morning to you too, John. Yes, we have some interesting finds." Danny remains quiet until the waiter has filled his cup and scurried off to a sufficiently distant table. "Our tails produced some interesting results, but nothing definitive. Monitoring the Carbonara HQ, however, may have given us what we need." Danny lays several color photos on the table depicting a large, suburban parking lot adjoining a tall, commercial building.

John studies them briefly. "What exactly am I looking for?"

"See the green Mercedes-AMG? Nice wheels if you can spare a couple hundred G's. I found it parked there four of five days last week."

"Member of their executive team?"

"Nope. This is visitor parking. Employees have their own lot. I ran the plates. It's registered to an R. Redder. Ring any bells?"

John's heart pounds. "That has to be Ramona. Carl's wife. She's a consultant with Interthon."

"And apparently, a highly compensated one."

"You've found it, Danny. She is the missing link. This makes perfect sense. It's exactly what we need!"

"Remember, John, a court would still call this circumstantial."

"I don't care!" John is out of his seat, grabbing the photos and heading towards the door.

Danny calls after him, "I guess you won't be staying for breakfast."

CHAPTER 27

The Executive Conference room at Victech has been prepared. Coffee pots and symmetrically arranged pastries await the attending Board members. Katy arrives first among the investors and since they had been able to connect last night, John quickly takes her aside to learn what transpired in yesterday's meeting of the V.C.s. "Do I still have a job?" John asks her.

"Barely. It almost went down. Carl wants you out now. Dick also. Not surprising since he sees himself as Carl's protege. Ed said he was leaning with them to remove you which would have been the end of it. But at Ed's insistence, it was agreed the vote would be postponed pending today's meeting. However, I spoke to Ed briefly earlier this morning, and it sounds like he's had a change of heart and would vote against removal. Not even sure Carl knows yet. I have no idea why Ed flipped. You didn't talk to him, did you?"

"No, I haven't spoken to him. And, by the way, thank you for supporting me."

"Too early to thank anybody," she grins. "You've got some serious 'splaining' to do."

They take their seats. The other Board members are filtering into the conference room and are soon seated. John had debriefed Tim before the meeting, knowing he would be attending both as a Director and in his capacity as Company Counsel. Normally, the Chairman would call the meeting to order and then turn it over to the CEO for the Management presentation, but today, Carl elects to conduct the meeting as an inquisition and has no interest in relinquishing control. Upon calling the meeting to order, Carl jumps right in.

"As investors and preferred shareholders, John, we are here to tell you that we have grave reservations, not only about the current financial status of the Company but also your performance as its Chief Executive. To begin with, however, we want to understand why you introduced a product plan to Board members that appears to be bogus. Is there or isn't there a company initiative to invest in developing Virtual Reality tools? Yes or No."

"No. That would make no sense for our market."

Waving the faux brochure with one hand, Carl continues, "And yet, you distributed this document to Board members, explicitly identifying VR tools as a key component of our product roadmap going forward. Is this correct?"

"Yes."

"Please, tell us why."

"Glad to. We have had a serious problem with leaks for several years now. These leaks have compromised our ability to gain a meaningful lead on our competitor, who likes to preannounce products which we have yet to bring to market and ones they haven't even started developing. As you once pointed out, Carl, it suggests we have a mole who is privy to our advanced plans. You knew I would never authorize polygraph tests. The VR plant was a way to narrow the search for the mole."

"Who all has this document?"

"Just the Board and the two senior executives who created it. They were sworn to secrecy."

"And why would you target the Board with this ruse?"

"Because I couldn't come up with a scenario where one of my team members would leak it."

There is an audible gasp from the room.

Clearly offended, Carl raises his voice, "You are on thin ice, John. Lying and providing false information to the company's owners constitutes cause for termination—"

John interrupts, "No one has asked me if we learned who the mole is."

Taking the bait, Dick asks, "Did you find out who it is?"

"Why, yes. As a matter of fact, we did, and thanks for asking, Dick! We have learned that the mole is Carl and his wife, Ramona, who works for the Interthon Associates Consultancy. Her client is our main competitor, Carbonara."

There is dead silence for a few seconds before Carl responds, "You don't know what the hell you are talking about! You cannot make an allegation like that without proof and citing proprietary information you don't have access to. This is slander."

Tim is prepped and jumps in on cue at the mention of

there being no proof: "The Company believes there is no other possible path from the date of the limited distribution of the VR flyer to the date that Carbonara announced their own VR plan. It was almost immediate. And that is why Victech intends to file suit against its Chairman Carl Redder, Ramona Redder, and RashCap Ventures."

Dick is visibly shaken, not able to contain himself. "Can this be true? Why, Carl? Why would you possibly want to do this? These leaks damage you directly as a Victech investor. How could any reward that your wife would receive from spying on us possibly justify the damage you're doing to our investment?"

"It can't," John responds. "The big win for Carl and Ramona was going to be when Carbonara bought us on the cheap for our customer base and technology. It will be interesting to see what sort of agreement Ramona has struck with Carbonara outside of Interthon. Personally, I can't wait for the subpoenas to start flying."

Carl is seething. "I have done nothing wrong. Nothing. You will all regret ever launching this attack."

"Carl, you are a fucking fiduciary," Tim says. "You have a duty of loyalty which you have breached. Go ask your own firm's lawyers how far they will defend you once we prove you intentionally betrayed your legal obligations."

Carl stands, red-faced and huffing. "You have no idea what the hell you are doing. Do you comprehend the scope of my enterprise? This company is chump change. It is expendable. You have made an irreversible error and one you will regret for the rest of your lives." He storms out of the conference room.

John does his best to hold the air of triumph he feels inside. He looks around the room and sees confused faces still absorbing what has happened, but he also senses a wave of relief washing over everybody. He has done it. He has found the long-time mole in Victech and saved both his company and his job in the process.

CHAPTER 28

Lynn and John enter the screened porch that faces their backyard. The night is still, and the early fall evening retains enough warmth to enjoy it. Lynn pours the wine as John sets up a Bluetooth speaker.

"So, it's a music night?" Lynn settles into her chair. "I thought you might want to reflect on your high drama today."

"That's the last thing I want to think about right now. Tonight's word is 'escape.' Prepare yourself for some special entertainment."

She mockingly begins to slow-clap. "Oh– you are going into D.J. mode? You haven't done that for a while. What is the musical theme tonight, Mr. Deejay?"

"First of all, Madam, I consider myself a musicologist who specializes in rare patterns in the historic music of the rock and roll era. I am not a 'Deejay' as you so crudely put it."

"Cool. So, what's the theme tonight, Mr. Musicologist Deejay?"

"I call this 'The Missing Verse' selection. Versions of songs that include a rarely-heard verse that did not appear on the original studio release."

"And why didn't they appear?"

"Excellent question. The artist may have decided it was too intimate. You tell me after you hear it."

"Intimate? Goody, I like it already," she says, slow clapping once again.

John queues up the home demo version of Tom Petty's "Crawling Back to You" and plays the missing verse. It describes a woman holding him like a child. She vows they will fight their nemesis to the end.

Lynn is impressed. "Wow, that's really powerful."

"What do you think it refers to?"

"Addiction. She's promising to help him break free and get clean."

"Nice work, I think so too." John queues another track. "Next one is tougher. This is Bob Dylan's "Sara" - a song about his long-time wife, but this version contains an alternative lyric." John plays the verse which describes the couple sleeping in the woods where she fought for his soul with God-like strength.

"Aw, that's sweet," says Lynn.

Nonplussed, John asks, "What do you mean? I really didn't get a bead on this one."

"It's sex, dear. She's teaching him the ropes. At some point, all you young men need instruction from someone more experienced."

"Hmm. Maybe. Are you good for more?"

"As long as the wine holds out. Lay it on me."

John queues a version of Simon & Garfunkel's "The Boxer" and plays the extra verse. It describes the years rolling by and how after many changes, the singer is more or less the same person.

As the music plays, Lynn's expression darkens suddenly. She shouts, "Wait! I heard something."

Both rise to their feet.

"I don't hear any—"

"Shhh! Hold it. Stop the music!

Still unsure of what is happening, John lurches to shut the music off. He steps off the porch into the yard to look around. He doesn't hear anything but crickets chirping for several seconds. Then, there it is. A strange, muffled screeching sound. John is puzzled, "I wonder what—"

"It's Maddy!" Lynn bolts into the house and up the stairs with John close behind.

***

They find the girl sobbing and screaming into her pillow at the top of her lungs. Lynn pulls the pillow away and hugs her breathless daughter, surprised at how forcefully the girl is hugging back.

"What is it, sweetie? What's wrong? Are you hurt?"

"She took something!" Maddy screams through her tears. She's gonna die! I'm so scared!"

"Maddy, who is going to die, and why? Calm down, and tell us exactly what you know," says John.

The girl chokes, sniffles, and sits up in bed. "My friend, Susan. We were on the phone. She told me she took some pills. I think she took too many. Her speech was getting hard to understand, but I told her to keep talking. Then, I think she must have fallen or something because she dropped the phone."

"What sort of pills?" asks Lynn.

"I don't know. Please don't let her die!" Maddy screams, sobbing again.

John dials 911. "I need Susan's address. Now."

Once the call is made and help is dispatched to her friend's house, John and Lynn have Maddy get dressed and come downstairs to sit at the kitchen table and tell them more about Susan.

"Tell us what led to this," says Lynn. "Did Susan ever try to hurt herself before?"

Maddy is still shaking but no longer hysterical. "No, but she hates her stepfather. Her real father died when she was four years old and her mother married this guy, Kyle. Susan says he is mean to her and to her mother. She told me he touches her in bad ways, and she hates it."

John and Lynn exchange glances. "Do you mean he touches her privately?" Lynn asks, waving her hand to identify her waist.

The girl nods.

"Susan told her mom about it, but she didn't believe

her," Maddy says. "Her mom told Susan she was lying just because she didn't like him. He hurts Susan every time her mom is gone. Susan is miserable. She told me she was going to run away."

"Maddy, did Susan say she wanted to kill herself?" John asks.

The girl began sobbing again. "Just on the phone call tonight. Just before she took the pills."

"Sweetie, why didn't you tell us?" Lynn softly asks her daughter.

"I promised her I would keep her secret. She's my best friend, and I promised her."

***

It would be almost two hours later when the police arrived at the Victor house and provided the family an update on Susan. They reported that medics had found Susan lying in the tool shed adjacent to her house, and Susan's mother, Melinda, claimed she had no idea her daughter was even missing from her bedroom when the squad car pulled in front of their house. The rescue team found her unconscious on the ground and laying in a pool of her own vomit. The empty pill bottle found nearby was a prescription for oxycodone, which Melinda admitted was hers from her back surgery a year earlier. The rescue team administered Naloxone, and Susan began to breathe again. The medics reported she should be able to make a full recovery from the overdose.

After receiving the update, the police then proceeded to question Maddy for over an hour, which included a more detailed version of the same narrative she had shared with her parents earlier.

When the questioning was over, John asked the Sergeant in charge, "What will happen with this Kyle character?"

"We have already advised Family Services that we have the suspected abuse of a minor," he responded. "An APB has been issued for him since we don't currently know his whereabouts."

It had become a very long and terrifying night. When the police finally left, Maddy's exhaustion took hold and she cried softly for another ten minutes, being consoled by her mother before she collapsed on her bed and into a deep and grateful sleep.

It is well after 3 a.m. when John and Lynn finally roll

into their own bed.

"Now, I understand what was behind Maddy's despondency," Lynn muses.

"We'll need to talk to Maddy about her keeping Susan's 'secret'."

"Poor Susan. I'm so glad she is alive. She must be traumatized. Her road back is likely to be a long one," Lynn sighs.

"Wow. This was one unbelievable night," John says in the quiet bedroom.

Lynn squeezes his hand under the covers. "Yes, but at least you were able to get away from all that office drama."

CHAPTER 29

John is buzzed from the front desk. "Jerome Asplund is here to see you."

"Send him in." John has been expecting Jerome since he contacted John late yesterday. It had only been forty-eight hours since Carl had self-detonated at the Board meeting and Carl's firm, RashCap, had already reached out with an olive branch in the form of another managing partner.

They shook hands. "Nice to meet you, Jerome."

"Call me Jerry, please. I appreciate you taking the meeting, John. I am one of RashCap's four founding partners. I am the "A" in 'Rash' if you will."

"Carl being the "R", I assume?"

"Correct. First, I wish to express my sincere apologies on behalf of the firm. You should know that Carl has been suspended pending an internal review. We are still gathering facts, but we believe there is nothing that justifies his gross misconduct as we understand it. His statements and position do not reflect those of RashCap Ventures."

"You know he sold us out to our competitor. Repeatedly."

"Yes, that is my understanding. Please know our firm had no knowledge of his conflicts. We were unaware of his wife's employment status or her clients. However, we have just learned that she is in possession of a written employment offer from this Carbonara firm for a top leadership position."

John nods, another puzzle piece falling into place. "Have you spoken with Tim?"

"Yes, we had an excellent call. My meeting with you here today is largely due to your counsel's insistence."

"Do you have proposed terms?" John asks. At least one proposed term is easy to guess: getting Victech to drop its planned suit.

"We wish to avoid any further acrimony and are open to your reasonable requests."

Over the next forty-five minutes, the men discuss the various concessions RashCap is willing to make if Victech does not pursue the lawsuit. For starters, Jerry would personally replace Carl in representing the RashCap seat on the Victech Board, at least for now. Any future substitution of the RashCap Director's seat would be subject to John's approval. RashCap would support Management's recommendation that Katy Curtis be anointed the new Chair which would also further diminish the powers afforded to the RashCap seat. Changes to the Investor Agreement would provide drag-along rights to assure RashCap could not obstruct a buyout offer, otherwise approved by the Victech Board and Management. Through a mutual, nondisclosure agreement, both parties would not initiate or support any adverse publicity about the other or details of this incident.

John finds Jerry to be friendly and open throughout the discussions. Coming to an agreement is especially important since John had recently learned that Victech's D&O insurance would likely not cover disputes or lawsuits deemed as being intra-Board. No need to share that tidbit with Jerry. So far, John is pleased with their progress.

"Jerry, I have two topics left on my checklist. Carl made a lot of threats on his way out the door. He is wealthy and extremely well-connected, and frankly, we wonder what he is capable of."

"Yes, of course. We cannot assume liability for his actions outside the firm," Jerry pauses before resuming. "However, I can share with you that Carl will soon be entering extensive negotiations with RashCap. A great deal hangs in the balance for him, including equity, future payments, and securing a neutral reference."

John struggles to resist laughing aloud at the concept of a "neutral reference" for Carl. Do words have any meaning at all?

Ignoring the flash of humor across John's face, Jerry continues, "Obviously, I cannot share discussions we may have with him in any depth, but there are certain claw-back provisions that can be enacted in case of future misconduct by Carl."

"Ah. Does misconduct explicitly include attempts at reprisal or retaliation against any parties associated with Victech or its Board?"

Jerry grins, "It certainly could. That works for us. We

will ask our lawyers to draft it accordingly. And the final topic on your checklist, John?"

"Had Carl not been so conflicted, we believe the investors would have re-upped their Victech investment this past year. Despite our growing sales revenue, he effectively blocked our access to new funding."

Jerry thinks for a moment. "Our perceptions of your company's status were all filtered through Carl's hidden agenda which we now recognize as corrupt. I cannot commit our firm to new financing at this time, but I can promise a clean-slate approach to rebuilding our impressions of your continued fundability. Let us get to know Victech better without Carl's misdirection. We are a quick study."

"Fair enough," John says, and the men shake hands. "Welcome to Victech."

CHAPTER 30

Lyra enters John's office. "Good news, boss!"

John looks up from his reading. "It better be. I hate when you call me that."

"We got the revised Aerie agreement draft back from Steve's people. Only one major change to the four-year version of our all-you-can-eat deal."

"Tell me it's not the price."

"Same price. Steve wants five years for the price of four—"

"Done."

"Wow, what took you so long?"

John is relieved and pleased. "Happy to hear it." He is

deep in thought and dives back into reviewing the newly revised draft from the RashCap lawyers to make sure all the concessions Jerry made at their last meeting have been correctly captured.

Oblivious to his preoccupation, a slightly hyper Lyra maintains one-sided banter, "So, the Sales team is actually ahead of schedule in ramping up. This is clearly the strongest group we've ever had. The Aerie deal gives us the needed ramp, plus some cushion. I predict we'll be swimming in Sales before year-end." Is he even listening? she wonders after not receiving a response. Not caring either way, she continues, "Marianne is over-the-moon with the cash flow. She said she'd trade her left nut to get a clean balance sheet."

This time, John responds without looking up, "So many reasons that doesn't sound like Marianne."

"Oh, you heard that? Good catch. You're right, she didn't say that. I did. But it had to be said."

"Did it?" John finally looks up and shakes his head. "Never mind. Back to Steve. Let's see if we can get this thing executed today."

"On it." Lyra turns and leaves the office.

In the hallway, Lyra becomes pensive. That was not the

conversation she had intended to have. A minute later, she stops walking and reminds herself that this has been put off too long. She doubles back to John's office, closing the door behind her this time.

John surfaces again. "What's going on?"

"I need to come clean about something. All this drama about Carl and his conflict of interest; such incredible dishonesty, and I... I need to tell you something."

"Should I be worried?"

She hesitates.

She has his full attention now. "Who did you murder?" he asks.

"Shut up. This is hard for me. You know I don't discuss my personal life, but I have been seeing someone for a while, and it's pretty serious. The reason I'm telling you this is... well, it's Ed."

"Duple? As in our Board member?"

Her voice grows shaky, "Yes. He and Trudy are separated, but full disclosure, this started before they were. Their marriage has been troubled for a long time. For a while, we were just friends, and I became sort of a confidant. But then it grew into something more. Much more. When the V.C.s were voting to oust you, I spent the evening persuading Ed to change his mind and support you, which is not ethical. I have been thinking about this a lot, and just like Carl—I hid the truth because I had a secret conflict. I was deceitful which is why I have been thinking the right thing to do would be to…"

"Stop right there," John cuts her off before she could utter the 'R' word. He cannot lose Lyra. "Think this through. Carl was actively working against the company he was supposed to be supporting. Your 'conflict,' as you call it, was a tactic to hold the company together. Very different."

Lyra's eyes grow moist as she speaks, "You have always been open and honest; frankly, a role model for my own career." John watches her, truly surprised. He has never seen her tear-up before. She is struggling for words. Hoarsely, she finally says, "I just feel I haven't lived up to that standard."

John sighs and speaks softly, "Listen to me, Lyra. I am not your dad, your husband, or your priest. I don't make judgements on your private life. Everyone has secrets— that's not what is important. Are your secrets malicious? Are they hurting people? I don't think so. That's what matters. You didn't compromise the company, Lyra. You did not." She is staring through him, seemingly into space, so he continues, "I rely on you and trust your judgement and intuition. I need you here with me. We must do this together. We are an unstoppable team."

There is further pause from Lyra, followed by a slight smile. She has processed his words and suddenly returns to Earth. She leans down and hugs John briefly before reverting to invincible Lyra again. "Thank you." She sniffles once more and then, it's over. "Let's not do this again, OK?" she says.

"Fine with me, but you may want to hear my hidden truth first."

"This should be good coming from the original Boy Scout."

"Hold that thought until you've heard me out. Danny, the detective I hired, showed me a series of photos he took of Ed's car. I couldn't help but notice, in many of the photos, it was parked outside of your apartment. So, I sort of suspected."

Her eyes widened. "You were spying on me?"

"Not you. He put tails on all the Board members and your place got picked up as he followed Ed's travels." She is staring at him, mouth open, so John presses on, "You were apparently snagged in an oversized net. Maybe think of it as friendly fire."

"Wow," Lyra mouths inaudibly. She is thinking all of this will blow the hell out of Rule #1. "I understand completely. It makes sense. I also think I owe you a fuck-you."

"Seems fair enough."

"Consider it said, then." She shakes her head, and heads for the door. "By the way," she adds from the threshold, "if you have any other hidden truths, please keep them to yourself."

CHAPTER 31

As the summer solstice approaches, the Victor family is determined to maximize porch time. John and Lynn are enjoying the long days and comfortable night air, talking quietly.

"I'm so relieved. Maddy's energy is back," Lynn says. "She is actually talking to Fredrick again—for the first time in months. I think she wants to ask him to the Sadie Hawkins dance next month."

"Good news indeed," John pauses thoughtfully. "You know our daughter showed some mighty bad judgement. Someone almost died as a result of her keeping a secret."

"All true. We've both been over that with her, and I know she gets it. But John, let's not miss the other side of

141

what happened. Everything she did was in empathy with Susan's situation. All the secrecy—it was her misguided way of being loyal and supporting her friend. Do you see that?"

"Hmm. As long as the word 'misguided' is included, I suppose. Yes, there is some type of integrity in there somewhere. Do we have any update on Susan?" John asks.

"Family Services has her in isolation for now. She called Maddy yesterday, but they were only allowed to talk briefly. They are trying to place her in a shelter home. She would love to see Maddy but doesn't know when it will be permitted."

"What about the stepfather?"

"The scumbag disappeared without a trace. Authorities are trying to track him down, though. Apparently, he wasn't really married to Susan's mom, Melinda. Not in any legal sense, anyways. The D.A. concluded Melinda was unaware of the abuse, if you can believe that. But Susan tried to report the abuse to Melinda who was in complete denial and never even looked into it. Because of that, she has lost custody of her daughter and is a total wreck. She needs to sort her own life out."

Maddy enters the porch wearing footed pajamas and

carrying a throw blanket.

"Aha, she lives!" John says.

"Hi sweetie, want to join us for a bit?"

The girl silently approaches Lynn on the oversized wicker chair. She curls up and nestles into her mother with the blanket.

John assumes his official Musicologist voice, "Well, you are both extremely fortunate to be here tonight as we have a special treat!"

Lynn sighs. "Here we go. Your father thinks he is a DeeJay."

"I call tonight's show 'Borrowed Lyrics.' These songs make no attempt to disguise the lyrics they have pilfered from older songs. We begin with Eddie Money's "Take Me Home Tonight," which not only features the lyrics from the original Ronette's song but includes a cameo from their lead singer as well." John rambles on before playing the song. He then moves on to Hootie's "I Only Want to Be with You," explaining its ties to a Dylan song called "Idiot Wind" while queuing the song. When ready, he turns back to his audience and sees both of his girls are sound asleep in the wicker chair, with one of them snoring just a bit.

"Wow," he says aloud. "Tough crowd tonight."

CHAPTER 32

It is November of 2022. John is a bit surprised by the invitation; not that Jerry hasn't requested John to join him several times in the five months since they first met for meals before, but this is a Hyde Park dinner, and Jerry requested it be a one-on-one without spouses. John infers that to mean all-business. Curiously, John can't think of any imminent Victech crisis to warrant a private pow-wow, though. This is intriguing, John thinks as he savors his filet mignon with onion straws and imbibes more Spanish Tempranillo. All are courtesy of RashCap. Warmup topics tonight, thus far, have encompassed golf, cycling, families, pets, and the weather. John is ready for Jerry's big reveal, whatever the hell it might be.

"We're thrilled by your string of sales wins, John. Looks like you're on a roll."

"Thanks Jerry. Yes, Lyra has really been driving the new sales team. Everyone's in the zone. Loving it."

"We have been discussing Victech's progress at the firm," Jerry says. "What do you think of buying out your investors?"

"Not the right time to sell the company, Jerry. We need to let the winning streak run. We're climbing to the next level."

"I completely agree. I'm just talking about buying out your institutional shares."

Huh? V.C.s only? John ponders this. "I don't understand. Why do you want to exit now?"

"It has to do with the way in which our funds are structured." Jerry explains that RashCap's portfolio companies, such as Victech, are grouped into funds. As is common for V.C. firms, there is a distinct set of Limited Partners investing in each fund. It turns out Victech was the last portfolio company added to RashCap Fund III. Venture funds have a limited lifespan, and the ancient Fund III needs to be wound down. Apparently, RashCap has been working to close it for several years, although that tidbit had never been shared with Victech.

It soon becomes obvious from Jerry's explanation that closing the fund is a matter of growing urgency within his firm. John gleans that some of its holdings may need to be written off as transactions with only modest gains or even losses. If Victech makes a proposal RashCap finds attractive, Jerry says he believes he can persuade the other Victech V.C.s to accept the offer.

John's head is spinning. "So, you're asking us to make you an offer to go away?"

Jerry grins. "If we can agree on terms, you can halt the dividend accumulation that weighs Victech down and take us off your cap table. It will once again be the John Victor company. Thanks to the Aerie deal and your strong sales performance, we think you are now in a cash position to take us out. The timing is right."

After further discussion, John promises he will raise the issue internally and circle back on whether Victech is inclined to proffer a buyout proposal. He thanks Jerry for the fine meal and heads for the parking lot to call Lynn. He did not see this one coming.

CHAPTER 33

Although the meeting had lasted less than an hour, Whitney Mitchell is exhausted. It is the third foster home she and Marcus have visited in recent weeks, and it has left both of them frustrated and disheartened.

"It's overwhelming, Marcus," she sighs. "So many of these kids, so damaged. Saddled with every kind of psychological problem and disorder."

"Did you catch what the director said about their ages?" Marcus asks her. "The average age of a waiting child in foster care is eight. Much of what these kids will become as adults is already baked in."

For the Mitchells, the meetings have been painful as well as instructive. They laid bare the horrors that push young children from their homes and into foster care. Addiction, abuse, incarceration, neglect, and crime are among the first memories to be imprinted on these young children. For Marcus and Whitney, the revelations are both shocking and eye-opening. Now empty nesters, the Mitchells' own experience in raising their daughter had been in a different world. It is their love of parenting that prompted Whitney to suggest they look into foster care.

The car ride home is mostly silent until Whitney speaks. "Perhaps we should revisit adoption?"

"We've been through this, Whitney," Marcus says softly. "It's an expensive and long-term commitment. Foster care is intended to be temporary until the child can be reunified with their biological family, which is often ideal. By contrast, adoption seeks to create a new family through permanent placement."

"You're making good money these days. It's one of the reasons you joined Victech and came in from the cold as a consultant. And your fulltime employment better qualifies us. We can afford it now."

"I'll put it as delicately as possible, dear; we are not young anymore."

"Speak for yourself, dear."

CHAPTER 34

John has convened the Victech senior staff and asked Tim to join the in-person meeting. After debriefing the group on his dinner with Jerry, he opens the floor for discussion and questions.

"Why are they doing this? Tax purposes?" Marcus asks.

"There is some of that but also, the optics. Closing old funds is window dressing," Tim explains.

"When they sell Limited Partners on buying into a new RashCap fund, it doesn't look good if the prior funds are still holding portfolio companies over seven years old with no exit in sight," John elaborates.

"We have a decent cash cushion for once, but I would hardly call us flush," Marianne says. "We are borrowing against future revenue from Aerie for five years. That's not a repeatable trick. Why would we want to spend our precious cash buying back their equity?"

"There are some distinct advantages," John says.

"Depending on the negotiated price, we could dispose of our accumulated and recurring dividend liability once and for all."

Tim nods. "It would be nice not having that boat anchor around your necks. It would also make the company's financial profile more attractive to future suitors."

"I completely agree," John says. "Also, all remaining shareholders and option holders, which include most of our employees and Jeffrey's old group, will experience negative dilution, so they will own a larger share of the company. That can mean a great deal in a future exit."

Marianne is not sold. "Is it really worth re-impoverishing ourselves for some hypothetical, future event? My sleep patterns have just returned to normal."

There are laughs around the room. Everyone knows about Marianne's dysfunctional sleeping habits.

"We need to be bullish on our current market position," says Lyra. "We are closing more and on larger sales, faster than ever before." She turns towards Marianne, "Our new release, 5.0, contains features our customers are awaiting and which are outside the scope of the multi-year Aerie deal. So, we will see fresh revenue from them as well."

"We won't impoverish ourselves, Marianne," John confirms. "I promise. We'll determine the limit we can afford for the buy-out and not exceed it. Hopefully, we can stay well under it."

After some further discussion, John assigns himself, Marianne, and Lyra to work the numbers and asks Tim to cobble together a template to construct a formal offer.

***

Naturally, the sticking point is the accumulated dividends. In his written response to the formal offer, Jerry tries to be as encouraging as possible, thanking John's team for their excellent good-faith progress, and praising the overall approach of the offer. But he makes it clear that the V.C.s see the dividends which have accumulated for the past seven years as debt unrelated to their equity stake. His written response says that John's proposal of simply wiping the dividends off the balance sheet is a non-starter.

John knows a more direct discussion is needed, and although Jerry is traveling, he agrees to partake in a Zoom call. After brief formalities, John insists they will need some sort of relief from the dividends. The conversation soon turns blunt.

"John, we view the accumulated dividends as our money in the bank. It's more like a loan."

"It's obviously not real debt, Jerry. It's part of your total return. Are you not treating this as carried interest for tax purposes?"

Jerry suddenly grows annoyed. "I don't know what the hell the tax treatment is, John. What I know is that you signed up for dividend accumulation at a fixed interest rate."

"8% compound interest is off-the-charts, Jerry."

"Maybe now, but it was appropriate for our risk management when we invested."

"It should have been tapered down or ended as our value continued to grow."

"But it wasn't, was it?" says Jerry, his anger clearly rising.

Both parties sense the risk of the negotiation degenerating further.

After a moment, Jerry collects himself. "Let's talk about how we might resolve this instead."

"Would you consider some sort of adjustment in the interest rate?" John asks.

Jerry sighs. "I don't know. I doubt it. The devil is in the

details."

"Alright. Let me take this back to the team and see if we can come up with something more creative."

"OK, John. Thanks. Talk soon," Jerry abruptly ends the call.

CHAPTER 35

Home has ceased to be the refuge it had been for John. Rolling in late and exhausted after another long day, he is greeted by an angry, stressed, and frustrated Lynn, who has spent too many hours building the case in her mind that her husband has abandoned his family.

"Is Maddy still up?"

"Of course not. Your daughter went to bed over an hour ago, heartbroken. She was hoping you would show up for her dance recital today. Just like last time."

"You knew I couldn't get back that early. Didn't you tell her?"

"I'm sick of explaining why her father is never here

during waking hours."

John does not relish this fight and has no interest in responding to her hyperbole. He heads to their wet bar to pour a drink.

Lynn follows him, continuing, "I didn't sign up for this, John. To be a single mother. You're never here. Your daughter is growing up without a father."

John bristles, "Come on, Lynn. That's just not fair. I'm trying to regain control of my own company. You know how important this is."

"When does it end, John? What are the limits of that excuse? She'll start driving in a year. We don't get these years back." The dam bursts, and Lynn is now yelling. "You're missing her whole life and ruining mine in the process!" She turns, leaving the room and climbing the stairs. The loud slam of their bedroom door rattles the house.

John sips his drink thoughtfully. Someday, I hope to have just one crisis at a time. I'll call that a vacation.

CHAPTER 36

The girl sitting across the table from Whitney and Marcus looks much older than her sixteen biological years. Unusually tall and physically mature, she could pass for twenty. But Whitney detects a weariness in the young girl's face and a sadness behind her eyes.

"We are so happy to meet you, Susan," says Whitney. "Marcus works with John Victor. We understand you are friends with his daughter, Madison."

The girl briefly perks up at the sound of her friend's name. "Yes, Maddy is my best friend." She hesitates, then adds, "Was. I don't get to see her anymore being in here."

"How is it here at New Path?" Marcus asks.

"It's OK. I miss my friends and school."

From the first time John informed Marcus about Susan and her history, he and Whitney did their homework to learn as much as they could about her. During a lengthy meeting with Ted Jenkins, president of New Path Foster Home, the couple spent time studying Susan's background, including her abuse at the hands of her mother's live-in boyfriend.

"Susan is not doing well in terms of integrating into our little family," Mr. Jenkins had explained. "She is isolated and depressed. She has very little interaction with the other fosters. We recognize her innate intelligence, but she has trouble concentrating. Susan is in her own shell and is terribly introverted. It is our judgement that attempting to introduce her back into a high school with her peers, at this time, would be a mistake."

"What is happening with her mother?" Marcus had asked.

"Her mother wants Susan back, but Family Services believes the mother is unfit and not able to provide a stable home for her. Susan needs a safe environment."

Those had been among the key insights from Mr. Jenkins, and now, with Susan sitting here in front of

Marcus and Whitney, they see it for themselves. The girl is so painfully despondent; just talking to her was bringing Whitney great sadness.

Marcus says, "Susan, if you had one wish, what would it be?"

Susan stares blankly and shrugs.

"Somewhere you would like to be? Something you'd like to be doing?"

"I don't know."

The Mitchells smile at her empathetically. There is a long silence. The girl is withdrawn and unable to converse well. They spend the next twenty minutes trying to draw her out more in conversation, but eventually, a staff member signals them the meeting must be wound up as it is the dinner hour.

"Thank you, Susan. We have so enjoyed meeting you," Marcus says. He and Whitney stand and prepare to say goodbye.

Susan suddenly asks Whitney, "Will you be coming back?"

The question is neutral, but Whitney hears something that sounds like an imploring quaver in the girl's voice. Surprised, Whitney reaches across the table and puts her hand on Susan's. "Yes, sweetie. We will return. I promise."

***

At their home that evening, the discussion is more direct. Prior to Susan, neither Marcus, nor Whitney, had previously considered fostering or adopting a teen.

Whitney says, "This is not what we discussed or what I had envisioned either. I saw myself parenting a young child. I guess I assumed maybe three to eight years of age."

"As we have learned, the older ones are the hardest to place," Marcus replies.

"Yes, and suddenly, they become adults and are set adrift without a home base. That child needs a home, Marcus. Why not ours? Would we consider adopting a teenager? We're not too old."

"Our age isn't the only issue, Whit. To state the obvious, this is a white girl. Having parents of color would present its own adulthood challenges, and those are challenges she never asked for. Would that be fair?"

Whitney responds without hesitation, "Yes. It is a fair price to pay to have a loving family. That's the most important consideration."

CHAPTER 37

"The sides won't reach," declares Marianne bluntly. "Too far apart."

She hands out copies of the summary report to John, Tim, and Lyra to study the numbers. Marianne has recalculated the dividend accumulation using several levels of slightly reduced interest rate. This is precarious since she and John have agreed RashCap will not bear much flexibility in this area.

Tim looks up from the report. "Can we repeat our half-and-half deal we did in those thrilling days of yesteryear?"

John smiles wistfully. "That won't cut it this time, Tim," he replies. "It doesn't get us what we want. The objective is to free ourselves of the V.C. investors. Get them off the cap table, along with their preferences, dividends, and all. They can't be only halfway gone."

Over the past few weeks since Jerry first suggested a buyout, it has become obvious that John has grown much more enamored of this objective. Everyone in the room clearly senses this, which adds to the collective frustration over the gap.

"Marianne, how big is the miss?" Lyra asks.

"A few million more would preserve some operating cushion. I'd be happy with three to five."

Tim says, "How about a bank loan?"

John and Marianne exchange simultaneous glances carrying the same question. Really? Several years earlier, they had established a line of credit with Gohio Bank. Its purpose was primarily to help smooth cashflow that resulted from year-end sales. Customers learned to rely on Victech, like most tech companies, to offer better terms near the end of its fiscal quarter. This is especially true at year-end when it coincides with use-it-or-lose-it monies in the customers' own budgets. This is the tech version of "seasonality." But, Victech never approached the bank with the notion of taking on more debt. In this case, however, it would be replacing dividend debt with bank debt, which would be far less expensive, anyways.

John responds, "You may be on to something, Tim."

"We could call Julie at Gohio Bank. It will have to be a term loan, not part of the LOC," Marianne says.

Lyra is animated. She turns to Marianne, "Intro me to your bank contacts. We will sell them on our updated track record and sales pipeline. It's a great story. We can crush this!"

John says, "I'll take bank debt over V.C. dividends any day."

Marianne addresses the group, "These are stodgy bankers. Can you 'sell' them?"

John nods toward Lyra, "She can."

***

It's only been five days since the decision to contact Gohio Bank. Marianne and Lyra are heading back from the bank meeting, calling John from the car.

Lyra says, "We're good. Julie needs to secure internal approvals, which will take a few days, but she informally told us it's a done deal."

"Super," John says. "That's great. Now we need to finalize the counterproposal and get it to Jerry today."

Marianne asks, "What did we decide to use as the revised dividend interest rate?"

"Screw it. Leave it as it stands. It's too much of a hot button for them. We have a bank cushion now. It must be clear this offer is 'Best and Final.' Our only ask should be to stretch out the payment maybe six months."

"Sounds good. Be there soon," Marianne says.

Hanging up and reflecting on the transaction, John realizes how hungry he has grown to buy out his institutional investors. If it can be accomplished, it makes sense at this juncture. John has found clarity: If Victech is ever to exit, it must not be too cluttered up with dividends and investor preferences. Otherwise, the team that made it happen suffers undue dilution. If this buyout succeeds, it clears the way for a future exit, capable of rewarding him and his entire team. This is a long-term play and a rare window of opportunity. He must seize it.

The most famous fast-growth tech companies that go public will command huge valuations, so that the substantial monies earned by investors and intermediaries tend to get scant notice. Everybody wins big. But for every

Silicon Valley unicorn or other exploder, there are a thousand bootstrapped companies that succeed on a much smaller scale and only after many years. These organizations need to remain watchful of the cost they are incurring and the risk of their ownership eroding over time.

Driving home that evening, John finds himself feeling more hopeful than he has in days. His thoughts quickly shift to his situation at home. Now he must persuade Lynn that things will begin to settle down after they buyout the major investors. John cringes recalling their argument the other night. He knows it became far too heated, but he will find a way to calm the waters.

Upon his arrival home, Lynn is acting peculiar and his optimism is swiftly dashed. She tells him that Maddy is upstairs in her room, John hears her music blaring, and then Lynn asks him to join her in the living room. Her demeanor is dark. Her voice is soft and shaky.

"I've made a difficult decision, John, and I want you to hear me out before responding. I am taking Maddy with me to live with my parents, at least for the time being. My mother will help us. The extra support is what Maddy needs right now."

John listens and takes the time to digest what she says

before responding quietly, "Babe, this is a mistake. Please don't do this. I know you are angry, but things really are looking up…"

"I am not angry. I just want you to understand our daughter needs more than I can give her by myself at this stage of her life. If not from her father, then maybe with help from her grandparents."

"What do you mean? She has me…"

"John, you know exactly what I mean. She needs more of you than what you can give right now."

He starts to argue, but quickly realizes she will not be swayed. Instead, he asks, "And how long—"

Lynn interrupts, "I don't know. I don't know anything yet, except this is what I must do for myself and for Maddy. You'll have access to her whenever you have the time. I don't have any details right now; we'll work things out as we need to."

CHAPTER 38

Victech has succeeded in buying out the interest of its institutional investors. The return to these investors is modest, but because it exceeds the original investment, it is listed in their win column which actually makes it superior to their average investment. The dismal truth is that a high percentage of V.C.-invested companies go out of business. The top V.C. firms that accrue great wealth do so from a surprisingly small percentage of very big wins. Because it is a win, the farewells with Jerry, Ed, and Dick prove quite amiable.

With the buyout consummated, John has the opportunity to restructure the Board of Directors, consisting of just five directors now. Three are insiders:

John, Lyra, and Marianne, and Tim and Katy will be the outside directors. The latter two are not current shareholders in the company, although as an individual who invested alongside the V.C.s, Katy did receive her modest percentage of the buyout.

To secure the loan that allowed the buyout to occur, Gohio bank imposed several requirements, including an opportunity to profit from Victech's future growth through warrants issued by Victech. The warrants permit the bank to purchase up to a fixed number of Victech shares over the next five years. In addition to the warrants, Gohio required Victech's adherence to certain covenants. One of the covenants sets a quarterly minimum on new sales revenue. Sales are still going well, but on this particular month, a large forecasted sale has slipped due to customer-related delays. Just enough of a miss to trip the bank covenant.

John has never missed a bank milestone before but is keenly aware the loan agreement contains numerous potential penalties for a covenant "breach." More concerning are the many anecdotal horror stories of banks conducting "workout" sessions to threaten, scare, and harass businesses that commit the ultimate sin of missing a milestone. The loan agreements provide numerous ways for banks to extract their pound of flesh, even for minor infractions.

On cue, Gohio contacts Marianne and requests an in-person meeting to "discuss" the revised forecast with Victech executives, including its CEO.

On Friday morning at Victech, the meeting with the bank takes place consisting of John, Lyra, and Marianne. Representing the bank is their regular contact, Julie, along with her boss, a stern-looking senior VP named Jacob.

After formalities, Lyra leads the discussion of the sales forecast and describes the single sale whose delay is responsible for the missed revenue target.

When she completes the review, Jacob asks, "What is your level of confidence that this laggard client will close next month?"

Lyra says, "I am ninety-nine percent sure they'll close by then. They will close. I only score a client at one-hundred when we have the signed license in hand."

"If it closes as expected, what percent of the milestone will you have achieved?" Jacob asks.

"We'll be at one-hundred-and-fifteen percent of the target," Marianne says.

Julie recaps, "So, to summarize, this deferred sale tripped the covenant, but you'll be back on track by next month on a year-to-date basis. Is that accurate?"

All three nod in agreement.

Jacob looks at Julie and then grimly back to the group. "OK, I think that's all we need for now." He produces a half-hearted smile and extends his hand to John.

Thanks, and other pleasantries are exchanged all around. Marianne escorts the guests from the office.

Now alone, Lyra looks at John. "That's it? No penalties? No public lashing?"

John, just as baffled, says, "Surprises me too. I guess it depends on the bank and the team assigned to our account. Apparently, Gohio is one of the good ones. So, no lashings."

"That's too bad. It sounded like fun."

John shakes his head. "You are one sick puppy." He then asks, "How are you and Ed doing?"

"Super. His divorce has been finalized; Evil Trudy is out of the picture. We really are good. Ed is as happy to be off the Victech Board as I am to be on it." She hesitates, then asks, "Things going any better with you guys?"

John has kept Lyra apprised of his own situation, so she

knows Lynn and Maddy moved in with Lynn's parents last month. "Not really. I have forgotten how to live alone. Apparently, it is not my forte."

Lyra reads the angst in his reply and does not ask for specifics. "Sorry," she says.

"Thanks." John changes the subject, "You think we should have a company cocktail hour after work this Friday to celebrate the investor buyout?"

"That's a great idea. It is well-deserved and will be appreciated by all. I won't be able to attend, though. You may recall I've been asked to speak in Cinci at the Women's Business Association of Ohio."

"Ah, you're right; it's a big honor. Go knock 'em dead."

"That's the plan."

CHAPTER 39

Reserving the second-floor party room at J. Liu's restaurant in Worthington proves wise as dozens of Victech employees pounce on the Friday afternoon invitation. Many bring spouses, friends, and other partners purportedly in the Victech orbit. In addition to the open bar, a buffet line serves up a fine assortment of heavy appetizers.

John is pleased with the turnout and is pleasantly surprised by the guest appearance of old friend, Danny Thurmond, whom he finds at a high-top table surrounded by a drinking group that currently includes co-founder and former employee, Russ McGraw, as well as Tim and

Marianne. John can hear Danny regaling John's employees with tales of himself and John in their younger years.

John approaches and interjects, nodding toward Danny, "I don't know what crazy stories this man has been spinning, but I assure you all, they are just the delusions of a warped mind."

Danny is unphased. "Given a choice between witnessing a total solar eclipse or attending an affair where John is buying the drinks, I choose the latter. Can anyone guess why?"

"Tell us," Russ says.

"It's the rarer event."

There is laughter all around.

Based on Danny's recounting of his past with John, Russ now feels empowered to rewrite the history of Victech's founding and his two years in Victech. He launches into a boastful version of the early days.

Marianne taps John's shoulder and beckons him away from the table. He is more than happy to escape Russ' rendition of the past and follows her without question.

"John, I'd like you to meet my niece, Elaine St. James," Marianne says, introducing a young lady.

"Call me Laine," the woman says, extending a hand. "So

happy to meet you, Mr. Victor."

John smiles and shakes Laine's hand. The girl is alluring. He judges her to be maybe late twenties, blonde, tall, and slender. She's wearing black jeans with a business-like white blouse.

Marianne continues, not giving John a chance to return Laine's greeting, "Laine is part of the founding team of a new startup. She jumped at my offer to meet the CEO of Victech, so I know she's eager to tell you all about it."

"It's nice to meet you too, Laine," John is finally able to say. "Sure, tell me about your company."

"We're designing next generation interactive voice response for the Fintech industry built around AI technology."

John nods. "The OpenAI advances have triggered a gold rush. How far along are you?"

"In the design stage still. I was hoping to pick your brain about starting up a tech business."

Noise from the growing crowd swells, and John notices as a new clique organically forms close to them, including Danny, Ernie Chase, and Keith West, the new Sales Director recently hired by Lyra. Keith, also vying for John's attention, works his way to the front of the forming pack.

John's immediate focus is still Laine. "Pick away," he says. The others settle around them in a circle to tune in.

"OK. First question is, when is the best time to start up our marketing efforts?" she asks.

Keith jumps in, "New company? Creating materials for Sales should come first. We can't begin selling empty-handed."

"That's true, Keith," John says, "but the initial messaging needs to be defined before the sales process can be developed. What is your initial message for the market, and how do you plan to announce it? Those are the questions I would ask first."

"So, no marketing push until we have nailed down both the messaging and the sales process?" Laine confirms.

"Close. Once you have your initial messaging, you can use social media to tease the market in advance of the announcement; building interest and awareness in your new brand. The sales process involves trial and error which feeds back into refining the messaging."

"OK, I get that. Second question, what skill sets are needed that we don't yet know about?"

Once again, Keith jumps in, "I'm going with Sales Support. Full-time liaison between sales and the backroom nerds." He turns to Ernie, "No offense intended."

"None taken," responds Ernie. "It makes sense Sales needs someone to dumb down the tech for them."

John ignores the barbs, "That's a really good question, Laine, with a number of branches. I'll go with the need for the principals to be multilingual across specialties."

Keith is perplexed. "English, Spanish, Mandarin?"

"I don't mean multilingual literally. It's important to communicate deeply with Development, Support, Sales, Marketing, Finance, Legal, etcetera. Not just the jargon but the insight and understanding of what drives, scares, and motivates each. A quality assurance tester has a very distinctive perspective from a developer. A marcom pro sees the world quite differently from an account executive. And don't even get me started on legal."

The last sentence is inserted for the benefit of Tim, who has just entered the circle. He responds without missing a beat, "Just think of us as the ones who bail your butts out after you've made a hash of everything."

Laine continues posing her questions, consistently being interrupted by spectators floating in and out of the circle as the noise level and general alcohol-feed chaos in the room grows. Finally, she leans over to John and speaks directly into his ear, "I really appreciate you spending this time with me. There is so much I want to learn, but this probably isn't the best forum to be doing this."

"Quite right," he responds. "Perhaps we can schedule a time when you can stop by the office with Marianne, and we can chat some more."

"I wouldn't want to impose at your office, but yes, I'd like to find some way we can get together."

For the next half hour, John is swept into conversations with numerous associates and their significant others. Mostly social, some work-related. When the room finally begins to empty, Laine returns to say goodbye. "Looks like everyone had a good time," she says as attendees head for the exits.

"Yes, they are well-fed and lubricated to start their weekends."

"I'm taking off now and just wanted to thank you again for your time."

"I've enjoyed meeting you, Laine, and wish you luck with your new enterprise." John looks around. "Where's Marianne?"

"She left. My aunt is not a big party person. I told her I would Uber home."

"Where are you heading? I can give you a lift."

"You don't have to do that. I'm in Clintonville."

"It's no problem. Happy to do it."

"That's nice of you, thanks. Let me grab my coat. I'll be right back."

Danny appears out of nowhere, pulling John aside and whispers, "I heard you say you're driving that girl home. Do you know what the hell you're doing?"

"What? Seriously? She's the niece of my CFO and starting a company. She has requested some mentoring. Am I supposed to just let her Uber home?"

"What she is looking for is not mentoring, John. She has other motives; it's obvious, especially from her body language when she's talking to you."

"Spoken like a true detective, Danny. And a bit insulting too. I'm a married man with a teenage daughter. I am not pursuing that girl. It's a ride. That's all."

Danny sighs heavily. "You've praised my intuition in the past, John. Listen to me now. Your marriage is in trouble and you're hurting. You meet this pretty, fawning young thing who likes what she sees. But I know, you and Lynn, you're going to work things out. You'll be alright; your marriage will be alright. I'm sure of it. As long as you don't do anything to tear the fabric in the meantime."

"Laine knows nothing about my marital situation and none of those things matter here. Is it not possible that she actually respects what I have done with Victech and sees me as a business role-model?"

Laine has returned with her coat, preventing Danny from saying anything more. He wishes them both a good evening and heads for the door.

***

They are in John's car heading down the road and rapidly approaching Laine's house. They have been talking nonstop for the entire ride.

"OK, let me tell you about something that happened at my last company," Laine continues. "It was like three years in, things were humming, and Dev began to insist they be allowed to rewrite the entire app—from scratch. It started a big fight internally, but they finally got their way. The rewrite scope was huge. Everything ground to a halt after that, including new sales, since Dev was spread too thin to prioritize dozens of enhancements and fixes on the production product."

"Yep. It's a more common tale than you might guess," John says. "No one knows exactly what's required before the system is built since the market hasn't weighed in. The market cannot fully explain what it wants until it tries it, so the architecture may be off kilter based on the actual value proposition. By the time Development wants to rewrite everything, it really means the system is finally stable."

Laine lights up on that word. "Stable, wow. This is what you meant about being 'multilingual' by specialty."

"You got it," John says, as he pulls the car up her narrow, Clintonville driveway.

Laine turns to him, "I'm learning so much just talking to you. I have like a million more questions. Can you come in and chat some more?"

"Thank you, but I'll have to pass."

She leans in, moving her face closer to his. "Please. This is so much better than a noisy party."

John pauses, "You know, if you stop by the office, I would like to introduce you to Lyra Keller. She is a highly accomplished executive and frankly, is a great role-model for young, ambitious women in the tech industry."

"Why would I want to settle for her when I can get wisdom directly from the horse's mouth?" Laine swiftly leans over and kisses him on the mouth.

John gently pushes her back. "Nope, don't. Laine, I am a married man."

"My aunt told me you are separated. I really like you."

John makes a mental note to punch his CFO in the nose.

Laine tries again, "Look, I didn't mean anything by it. I'm not trying to jump your bones. Just come in for a bit more conversation. Maybe a drink?"

"This is just not happening. It was nice to meet you, Laine."

She stares at him momentarily, then looks down and quietly exits the car. "You too, John."

He drives off, crediting her for not resorting to an outburst. She is too smart for that, he thinks. Her smell and the softness of her young lips still resonate on a visceral level, but John will not allow himself to get drawn into that. He suddenly pulls the car over to the side of the road and sends a text to Danny: Thanks for your sound advice. Correct as always. Fabric remains untorn. You are a good friend.

CHAPTER 40

"Thank you all for coming today, and welcome to the forty-second quarterly meeting of the Women's Business Association of Ohio. I'm Neely Striker, Chair of WBAO. We have a special guest today, Lyra Keller, who is an Executive V.P. at Victech LLC based in Columbus. As you likely know, Victech is a rapidly growing tech firm and one of the great Ohio start-up success stories of recent years."

Over one hundred and fifty attendees are in the auditorium. Neely and Lyra have been provided with microphones, and assuming the moderator's role, Neely asks Lyra about her background, how she got her start at Victech, and what she has witnessed during her twelve-year tenure at the company. Afterward, Neely announces that she will now open up the floor. The audience is comprised of women from recent grads to mid-life career changers, and when Neely finally asks if anyone has questions for Lyra, several dozen hands shoot up.

Q: "You said you started in Marketing. Is that a good point of entry for Tech?"

A: "It's a personal choice. Marketing has always been home base for me. It's the test bed for determining if your innovation has value. Your messaging emanates from there. Technology often provides the creative starting point and creates the innovation candidate. The market either proves or disproves its value often depending on the effectiveness of the Marketing and Sales."

Q: "It seems like all the good ideas have already been done. How do you even get started?"

A: "Nothing new under the sun, right? It seemed that way five years ago. It also seemed that way ten and thirty years ago. Based on the innovation we've seen since we now know it was never true before, and it still isn't.

But how to get started? Begin with something you know, something you love, or something you believe in. Or even have an interest in. It could be in consumer products, manufacturing, healthcare, biotech, aviation, the arts, computer science, style, food, energy... Anything! Then ask, 'how can this be improved? What is needed here that doesn't exist?' Understand the broad nature of what technology can do. It can automate, amplify, replicate, or enhance. It can free humans from repetitive or rote tasks and improve productivity. Look at recent breakthroughs in AI. There will soon be thousands of applications building on this new power as it becomes better understood. Once we understand how to assure we can trust it, apps will build on other apps. What can AI do in your field of interest? What unsolvable problem can now be solved?

Here's another approach if you're not sure what you want to pursue: catch a wave! Ride what is actively trending and not just in the consumer market. Waves come from a number of sources. Government mandates create waves. In the case of business-to-business, mandates create needs for thousands of companies to fulfill new requirements and meet new standards. For business-to-consumer, popular culture also spawns its own form of waves."

Q: "What role do you see social media having?"

A: "Clearly, it always makes everyone's life so much happier!"

There is a mixture of both laughter and groans from the audience.

"OK, seriously. Like having a website, a presence on social media is a must-have for any company but it's role and importance can vary widely. In a B2C company, think consumer products, it may be the vehicle for nearly one-hundred-percent of sales and marketing efforts. But compare that to a B2B company with a smaller universe of serviceable customers, think maybe Fortune 500. In that market, you are better off with strategic selection and targeting of accounts. Where are your prospects? Are they best found online? There is no single answer for all businesses. That would make it too easy."

Q: "In the agenda, it says you describe your approach as 'Balls to the Wall.' What does that mean, and why in the world would you call it that?"

Once again, there is a rumbling from the audience. Neely tries to calm the waters: "It is well known that Lyra has a playful sense of humor…"

A: "It's OK, Neely, thanks. I've got this. First, 'Boobs to the Wall' doesn't work. Secondly, sorry if anyone was offended, but there really is an important point here. It's means drive and tenacity. I'm often asked which are the most important, personal characteristics required to succeed in a startup. One is your drive. In starting a business, you need to go at it hard. Aggressive in your pursuit and relentless in your ability to rebound, since you will encounter one setback after another. Trust me, you will. Male, female, whatever, it really doesn't matter. If you can prove the value of your product, with drive, you should be able to work your way through anything."

Q: "But what role does luck really play? Look at Zuckerberg, Bezos, Gates, Musk. All the billionaires. Are you saying luck has nothing to do with their success?"

A: "Quite the contrary. It's very simple: luck is necessary but not sufficient. The success stories all had their share of luck, but they also had the drive and tenacity among other personal strengths. We make our own luck. The expression is 'Luck is what happens when preparation meets opportunity.' You can improve your odds of being lucky just by being in the game and alert. Learn to recognize luck when you see it."

Q: "With all due respect, Ms. Keller, I admire what you have accomplished, but you're not even the founder of Victech."

A: "Quite true. I like to say Victech was a puppy just

past its paper-training stage when I started a dozen years ago. I was fortunate in being recruited by John Victor, who was an instant role model and who became a continuing mentor without even trying. When I shared my opinions on areas outside of Marketing, he gave me the room to maneuver and expand my skill set. Others would have told me to stay in my own lane and not attempt to branch out. There is room to flourish in a startup if you are given permission to try new things."

Lyra responds to questions for another half hour before Neely wraps it up. There is a strong and lengthy round of applause for Lyra. She is flooded by attendees after the meeting.

Driving back to Columbus from Cincinnati that evening, Lyra is exhausted but feeling good. She knows she is on top of her game.

CHAPTER 41

In the six months since Lyra hired him as Sales Director, Keith West has never been more upset. Henry Li closes his office door so they are not overheard.

"OK, tell me what happened," Henry says.

"Gladly. It's your new marketing rep. Kathy, is it? She's outta her fucking gourd. Did you see what she gave us for the 'Release 5' announcement?"

Henry has not seen it, which itself is surprising. He had brought on Kathy Amber as a junior marketing rep last month. Her first major assignment is to design the announcement for the big release of the showcase Victech product. Apparently, Kathy has created a radically new design and sent it to Sales as a done deal.

Without awaiting a response, Keith opens his laptop and presents Kathy's creation to Henry.

"Oh dear," Henry immediately reacts. "This is off-brand."

"That's the least of its problems," Keith says. "It's outrageous. It's Frankenstein. The colors are not ours, the logo is distorted, and she even modified the copy we gave her. The copy! It is not her job to rewrite the fucking copy. So, I confronted her on Slack, and she became unglued."

This is not the auspicious start Henry had foreseen for Kathy. "Tell me, what exactly did she do?" he asks, not entirely sure he wants to hear this.

"She told me I am only Sales; that she is the Creative, and her work is not subject to my review. She says that she owns this piece and Sales does not. When I told her she needs to work within the guidelines of our brand and the messaging we provide, she started screaming at me about how many hours she has worked on this design last week."

"How did you leave it?"

"I don't deal well with hysteria, Henry. I ended the Slack call."

"OK, Keith. I will speak to her and circle back."

"Thanks, Henry. I should mention, we need the

announcement to go out by Monday," Keith says. He adds with a wry grin, "No pressure, though."

***

As privately advised by Marcus, Henry requests an in-person meeting with Kathy in his office. The objective of the meeting is to determine whether Henry thinks Kathy is salvageable. The next steps will depend on that determination.

He speaks first, "Keith West described an altercation he had with you. I would like to hear your perspective."

"Sales people are uninspired. You can't expect them to grasp a bold, new approach. I tried to explain to Keith that creativity must not be tied down if the organization is to thrive."

"You do know Victech already has an established brand and detailed brand guidelines, correct?"

"Yes, and designated primary and secondary brand colors, and logo usage, and size guidelines, blah blah blah. Please tell me you don't want your marketing team to be trapped inside that tiny box."

"We have a widely respected and admired company

image, Kathy. Our best work is collaborative. It pulls in the necessary elements from sales, marketing, finance, etcetera to nurture and reinforce that image."

"I own the design for this announcement, right? Did you not assign it to me?" Kathy's tone grows more challenging.

"I assigned you a piece of an important collaboration. It has to work for Sales, and it must be compatible with how Victech is perceived by our customers."

Her eyes are now darting like a trapped animal. "I want to talk to your boss, Lyra. She runs both Sales and Marketing, right? She should have the final say on which side is favored. Also, she is not a man, so there'd be less bias toward your side."

"That's not going to happen, Kathy. This is not a contest between departments. I told you our work must be collaborative. Also, you don't work for Lyra. You work for me." Until you don't, Henry is thinking.

It gets easier from here. Henry has concluded she is not salvageable. Marcus has provided the rest of the termination script.

***

Henry reaches Lyra by phone as she is driving back from Cincinnati.

"So, what happened?" she asks when she picks up.

"My new hire, Kathy, totally butchered the design for the release announcement. It was a dog's lunch. Wrong colors, wrong logo, wrong copy. Irreparable."

"Ugh."

"Sales puked all over it, and she got into it with West. Threw a tantrum when I confronted her about the need for collaboration."

"And the actual announcement?"

"We're covered. I rejiggered my group's priorities. We'll have it by Monday."

"Super. And our prima donna?"

"Gone. Marcus helped me with the termination."

"Appreciate the agility, Henry. Also, I appreciate you resolving this without pulling me into it. Good job."

CHAPTER 42

The 9:00 p.m. FaceTime call has become a nightly ritual. Maddy describes her day to John before he talks to her mother. Tonight, she tells her father about school and the most exciting things going on in Maddy World. She is anxious to start studying for her Temporary Permit test which she'll be able to take when she turns fifteen and a half. Lynn and John have already decided it will be John who accompanies her for most of the fifty hours of driving she will need for the temporary license. Lynn says her nerves couldn't stand it. After other wide-ranging teen topics, John asks if she is getting along with Grandma Marsha.

"Grandma is nice to me, dad, but she and mom argue a lot." She pauses, then says, "When can we move back with you at home? I hate it when you're not with us. This is all mom's fault."

"That's not true, Maddy. Don't say that. Your mother wants what's best for everyone."

"She took us away from you. I just want things back like they were." He hears her start to cry. "When can we all live together again?"

"You will see me a lot, Maddy. Your mother and I are working things out. Please, be patient with us. It'll be OK."

After a few more minutes, he says goodnight to Maddy and ends the FaceTime call before calling Lynn back audio-only, since she had told John she doesn't like talking on camera. They review a number of living necessities, coordinating on issues with bills, house maintenance, and pickup and handoff times for Maddy.

Following their review of the essentials, John asks, "How are you and Marsha getting along?"

"It's working OK. She relieves me of a lot of the overhead. Doing the best we can." It's clear to John that living with her mother is not tenable for Lynn long-term.

"I want you to know that things are quieter now at

Victech. As unusual as it sounds, we've been running on an even keel."

"That's good. Have you been able to cut back on office time?"

"Not yet. But I am working on a plan that will drastically reduce demands on my time."

Lynn scoffs, but John presses on, "I want you back, babe. The three of us together at home again. I can make this work."

"OK, John," Lynn is not up for this conversation right now. "Later."

The call ends. In the empty house, John pours himself a drink and plays "It'll all work out" by Tom Petty. My new theme song, he thinks.

Alone in a bedroom in her mother's house, Lynn tries to read but finds herself too distracted to focus. His great expertise is saving his company, she is thinking. Saving his family is out of his scope.

CHAPTER 43

Fourth quarter marks the time for finalizing next year's plans and budget. Once again, John and Lyra are lunching at Hunan Lion where all great plans seem to be hatched. They have been discussing their upcoming hiring requirements and the new budget. The process has become immeasurably easier without institutional investors involved. Fewer iterations and approvals are required for major decisions. The smaller Board is now comprised of insiders and friends, allowing management greater agility in making and enacting decisions. Although the company has grown considerably, for John and Lyra, it feels leaner and more streamlined than it had been before the buyout.

"Another topic I'd like to raise," Lyra is saying: "Should we consider retiring our bank debt? We have the cash and cashflow to do so."

"I don't think so. For one thing, it's relatively cheap money by today's standards. Also, we don't have many ready sources should we encounter another crunch. From our experience with banks, it seems prudent to pay a little interest to keep the bank lines lubed and ready."

"Sure. Nicely worded too. How about if we retire some of it just to keep the balance sheet shiny?"

"Hmm. That might make sense. Talk to Marianne."

Lyra nods.

After a pause, John says, "I also have a new topic I would like to introduce."

"Uh-oh. I'm having a déjà vu moment," Lyra says. "Tell me it isn't another of those John Victor bombshells. I really don't want to do another VR brochure."

"Katy asked me recently whether I had a succession plan. I currently do not."

"Succession? You think there is a semi with your name on it?"

"I am looking to reduce my level of involvement in the

Company, perhaps over the next six months. As part of that change, I want you to become Victech's new CEO."

Lyra is stunned into silence for a three second eternity. She then replies, "John, I am incredibly flattered, but, and let me put this delicately, you are just not that old."

"That's not the point. You are aware of my personal issues. I need to reunite my family by spending more time as a spouse and father. I have been derelict in the time I have afforded them. Especially in recent years. The only way to fix this is by devoting more of my time and energy to my family." She starts to reply, but John holds up his hand and continues, "I plan to stay on in a diminished role as Chairman. Still there to backstop you. But let's talk about you. Over the last decade, you have mastered every aspect of this business, including sales, marketing, support, finance, and development. You are enormously respected by the team, customers, and partners alike. You are uniquely qualified to run this company. We can phase you into the role starting around the middle of next year. What do you say?"

Lyra chooses her next word carefully, "Gulp."

"You know you know you can do this."

"I am beyond intrigued, but I also have to work through

some things in my personal life." She lowers her voice and continues quietly, "I'm a thirty-four-year-old single woman who has never had a child, and am living with a wonderful man who has two grown children himself. I'm also an unapologetic workaholic who loves what she does, but I'm just beginning to reflect on the life-decisions I've made so far. I don't want to ever look back and regret the path I have taken. Bottom line: I want time to consider this remarkable opportunity you are describing. That means time to think and also to talk with Ed."

"Of course. Take all the time you need," John says. He wants and hopes she will say yes, while concurrently being fully sympathetic with Lyra's needing to weigh her options.

"But regardless of where this goes, I am thankful for your offer. I mean that profusely. I really am honored."

CHAPTER 44

It is a chilly Saturday morning, and John is in his car with Maddy behind the wheel. One day before her sixteenth birthday, she has made tremendous progress since she first drove with her father weeks ago, following her completion of Driver's Ed instruction. Today, John is giving her specific turn-by-turn directions without identifying the destination.

"Where exactly are we headed?" Maddy asks after about twenty minutes of driving.

"It's a bit of a surprise. Don't you like surprises?"

"I just want to know where we're going, dad."

"At the next street, turn right. There will be a driveway

a couple of houses down; pull into it. I'll point to which one when we're close enough."

"Very suspenseful, dad. And whose driveway am I am turning into?"

"Do you remember the Mitchells? Marcus and Whitney? He works at my company and you've met them at our parties in the past."

"Sort of. And why are we visiting the Mitchells?"

"To congratulate them on the newest member of their family."

After she makes the instructed turn, John points to a driveway that leads to an elegant, colonial style house. Maddy pulls up the designated driveway and turns off the ignition. She turns to her father, "Did they have a baby?"

"Even better—" says John.

Before John can finish his sentence, the front door of the house opens, and Marcus and Whitney step out. Standing between them is a tall, smiling sixteen-year-old girl.

In less than a second, Maddy is unbuckled and out of the car, running up the driveway and screaming, "Susan!" They embrace and continue screaming in unison out of excitement.

"—they adopted," John says, inside the now-empty car.

***

Whitney and Marcus are dumfounded by the fervor of Susan's reunion with Maddy. In the short time she has been under their custody, they have not seen her exhibit such energy and excitement. The new adoptive parents are both delighted and stunned. To nurture the happiness, they allow the girls to spend the afternoon together, and then Whitney invites John and Maddy to stay over for a cookout with them, to which John gratefully accepts. He sends Lynn a text to advise her that Maddy will be returning after dinner.

Despite the chilly air, Marcus hands John a beer as he tends the outside grill, packed with brats and burgers. "I swear it was a metamorphosis, John. Susan turned into a butterfly before our eyes."

"This is a part of Susan's prior life she never stopped craving. Maddy also. These two really missed each other," John reflects.

"Clearly. But it's still early days. Susan is acclimating to a new home and parents. I can't help but believe Susan's emotional reaction is healthy. Where do we go from here? How often should they be getting together?"

"Lynn and I will work that out with you and Whitney," John says. "The big question for you guys is, when will Susan be returning to school?"

Marcus sighs. "The foster home is on the record stating they are dead set against it. They believe she is too withdrawn. But they haven't seen the butterfly we just saw…" he trails off for a moment, lost in thought. "Whit and I agree; she needs to be back in school. She should have started in August. We plan to get her back in before she loses too much of the year."

"Well, just a heads-up, in case you haven't given it much thought, school means new clothes, shoes, books, afterschool activities, school supplies, and a computer… just for starters."

"Thanks, John. Got anything else to keep me up at night?"

"Yes, one more thing. She's also going to want to start Driver's Ed." Marcus' eyes widen. "Welcome to my world," John says, grinning.

CHAPTER 45

The December night is chilly, but the highway from Cleveland to Columbus is dry. Ed's Tesla speeds south on I-71. He and Lyra are returning from dinner with Ed's daughter, Madeline, a nurse at University Hospitals. Lyra makes the most of the two-hour drive and fills Ed in on the details of John's proposal from earlier. As she talks, he is brimming with excitement.

"Succeeding John as CEO of Victech. Sweetie, that's just fantastic! A huge and well-deserved honor. I am so proud of you. And John is right: you can do this."

"Thanks Eddie. I agree, it's a role I have been groomed for, but you need to understand, this is much bigger than just a job decision. My life is at a crossroads. Do you get that?"

"Yes, and I think it's about time you marry me. I've only been proposing to you for about three years. Are you ever going to say 'yes'?"

"As the magic eight ball says, 'reply hazy, try again.'"

She won't be pinned down, at least not now.

Ed shakes his head. "Thanks for that mature and thoughtful response. Fine. Tell me about your crossroads."

"Chief Executive is the top rung, of course. It is my career pinnacle and it's an all-in commitment. You know John has been an amazing mentor for over a decade now. This move should be my highest aspiration, and I am genuinely honored by the opportunity, but... I have also seen the demands of this position nearly consume him at times. Between us, Eddie, a key reason for him to promote me is to give him the space to save his own marriage."

"And you are concerned that we..."

"No, we are good. I'm not worried about us. That's not what I am struggling with." She pauses before continuing.

"I want to talk about children. You know we never decided not to have them as a couple. But instinctively, my reaction has always been not now. Push it off a little longer.

At some point, though, my path to becoming a mother will disappear. Poof. Bio-clock and all that crap. And now with John's offer, it suddenly feels like these deferred decisions are being thrown in my face. Decisions I must make now will lock in my destiny. The stakes just seem so high…"

"Let's not go off the rails. First, you and your bio-clock still have a long journey ahead of you. But, can you take a minute to appreciate how very full and blessed your life is? John selected you as a successor because of your independence, skill, and dedication. All things I love about you too. Now, you have the chance to run this company, which you helped build, by the way. Victech has long since outgrown the day-to-day survival mode of its past. Also, John is still around to back you up."

"I do appreciate all of that…" she begins, "but I don't think I've ever asked you directly, Eddie. Tell me how you feel about having kids." She raises her fingers to signal Rule #3: Painful honesty. "Clearly and bluntly, please."

He knows she will not be diverted and struggles to find the words. "OK, the blunt version is: been there, done that. I am eighteen years older than you, sweetie. Always have been, always will be. I've had my children and lived all those stages. From diapers through college and now, an empty nester. The whole, beautiful mess. It's true, there are some sweet memories in the mix, but you know my ex had no life to fall back on when the kids left home. The contrast can't be starker. You have a rich and full life now and ahead of you."

"Sure. I understand. I know you've lived through all the stages, but I never had those experiences, Eddie. Suppose I want the whole, beautiful mess? Must I decide today to foreclose the possibility of having children?"

"I am completely biased in this discussion, Lyra. I can only share my perspective with you. Unlike those years when I was raising my kids, I'm now living with my perfect life partner. Yes dear, that's you. You are the best thing in my life and all I could ever want from a relationship. What we have is a thousand times more appealing to me than reliving the child-raising years. I want us to make the most of our lives together. So, here is my heartfelt and totally selfish advice, embrace the honor you have earned. Take the top slot, dive in like only you can, relish the adventure, and let us not dwell on the road not taken."

CHAPTER 46

Other than during brief hand-offs of their daughter, it has been weeks since Lynn and John have met in-person. She resists John's insistence on meeting, not wanting to be worn down by his relentless imploring that she and Maddy return home. But I am worn down anyways, she now thinks as she drives to meet him. Living with her parents is no panacea. She must walk on eggshells to avoid confrontation with her mother, and even so, her mother's comments frequently seem intended to infantilize her, either because she still sees Lynn as a child or simply because she wants to provoke her. Neither one makes for a healthy home life.

The frustration probably explains how John was able to persuade her that a face-to-face meeting is needed. He had couched the reason in terms of it being a necessity they address numerous decisions about Maddy and the arrangement of their lives going forward. When she finally agreed to a dinner meeting, Lynn's plan was to don psychic armor by keeping the discussion at arms-length, but enroute now, she finds herself laden with overwhelming sadness. She has lost whatever appetite she had for rehearsing her husband's failures; she is too empty and too exhausted.

She arrives late at Firebirds restaurant in Polaris. John has scored a quiet corner table and ordered drinks by the time she walks in. A Mojito awaits her. She takes a seat, apologizing for her late arrival. Beyond the brief pleasantries, they soon tackle numerous updates, parental decisions, and observations as their discussion gains momentum. Among them:

☐ Marcus and Whitney provide a nurturing home for Susan who has missed the first few months of the school year. Maddy has offered to help her friend as she catches up. Both parents are pleased with Maddy for her effort in supporting her friend.

☐ The pandemic is no longer a major factor. Travel business is starting to pick up for Lynn. People are getting out more.

☐ Maddy turned sixteen last week. Lynn thinks she is okay with her taking the Driver's test when she reaches fifty hours of driving with a guardian. Maybe. John notes that Maddy is almost there and she's doing well in their practice drives. Lynn agrees she seems very road-aware and not reckless. Maybe.

☐ Lynn has grown inured to Marsha's many provocations and is no longer easily triggered. A delicate truce of sorts prevails in their daily interactions. However, her mother will always perceive her as some sort of eighteen-year-old airhead. John helpfully suggests it must be nice to be perceived as not aging.

☐ The new product release has had a strong start, and Victech sales are ahead of plan year-to-date. The company actually paid off a chunk of its bank loan early.

☐ Inflation is driving insane housing prices. A neighbor down the street just sold their house at a surprising premium. They both wonder how much is our house worth now? Demand will slow as interest rates rise.

Over drinks and dinner, John and Lynn spend the next

hour covering a multitude of issues, events, and questions of the sort couples share daily. From the ridiculous to the sublime. All things, great and small. The bath faucet upstairs drips. Budgeting for Victech has become much easier without second-guessing by V.C.s. Some incomprehensible warning light has appeared on the dashboard of Lynn's car. What must Maddy do next year to prepare for college application and selection. Having been starved for couple-level interaction, the two feast on all they have missed over the weeks apart. The pent-up sharing is replete with wisecracks and playful snark. Lynn finds herself smiling, even giggling, for the first time she can recall. It all feels so strangely normal.

The next words out of her own mouth take her by surprise, "I miss you."

John gasps quietly, "Oh, babe, you have no idea. Every hour, every day. I want you both to come home. Please, come home. I know how we can make it work."

Lynn responds, unveiling the thoughts she has carried privately for weeks, "Something I need to tell you that I should have said long ago, as a matter of fairness, it's just that, you and I are built so differently. I can't handle stress the way you can; it tears me apart. You thrive on it. It's not your fault, it's just the way you are, and I understand it really is a strength of yours. But it doesn't take much for me to get heavily stressed, and I cannot function when I am. My mind just keeps looping on the problem without making any progress." Lynn pauses before continuing, "The same stressors that spark you to action and creativity paralyze me. When there was no money coming in, when Russ quit, when Carl almost destroyed the company, he came damn close, when we couldn't pay off debt to the investors, when we were illiquid, when Aerie nixed your proposal, Susan's suicide attempt, and when I feared Maddy growing up without a father... You'd think I'd get used to these cycles, but as I get older, my level of agitation seems to be worsening."

John responds thoughtfully, "I understand, and you make a good point about how I work with stress. Remember Dick Greene, formerly of fame as one of our V.C.s? During the closing stage of the buyout, he made an interesting remark. He told me if I were half as good at growing the company as I am at saving it, we'd be Google by now. I don't think it was intended as a compliment."

"No question," Lynn agrees. "Your rescue abilities are uncanny, but I can't handle the thrill ride like you can. I'm becoming an old lady rattled by her nerves."

"Hardly old. According to Marsha, you've not yet hit puberty."

"Don't get me started. She'd be happy if I went back to pigtails."

"Babe, I understand and respect your need to minimize stress, and I know I have a key role in assuring that you do. I know how to make that happen. I actually have news I need to share. I've made the decision to retire as CEO of Victech and pass the baton to Lyra."

Lynn is stunned. "Seriously? But why? Victech is your life. John, you're not even fifty yet. Why in the world would you leave it?"

"You, me, and Maddy: I want us to be a family again. That's why. I will still be Chairman, but I will phase down to forty hours a week or less."

"This is amazing and unexpected news. You are amazing. I don't know what to say. But John, you have dedicated most of your adult life to building this great company. Victech is you. This is what you do—it's what gives you purpose. I cannot be responsible for you losing all of that by letting you walk away."

"I am not walking away or losing it. I will still be

attached to the company and its largest shareholder. But I am taking the necessary steps to regain my family, which is my priority. Victech is not my whole life. You may recall you knew and married me before there even was a Victech. So, there must be more to me than the Company."

***

Central Ohio nights in mid-December are bleak. Tonight, a cold Wintry wind howls outside amid blowing snow and bad roads. A level two snow emergency has been declared for Franklin and most adjoining counties.

Within the cozy bedroom of their house, Lynn softly asks John, "Are you awake?"

"Um. Yeah. I did fall asleep briefly. Best reunion ever."

Her head rests on his chest. In the darkness, John can sense her smiling. "One hundred percent," she says.

"Did I mention last night you're even more beautiful than I remembered?"

"No, you were too busy tearing my clothes off."

"You were tearing mine off too."

"Just trying to keep up."

"Ahh." John adds, "It's nice having the whole house to

ourselves."

"Definitely. Maybe Maddy should stay at her grandmother's place permanently."

"Yeah, I love that idea."

"Now, isn't this better than your idea of finding some cheap motel?" she asks.

"That just sounded like an adventure. But this is cheaper. Already paid for, you know. Slightly less scuzzy too."

"Sure. Also, lower bedbug count, which is a definitely a plus."

"I knew that would woo you," he said.

"Is that what you did? Did you 'woo' me?" she yawns.

"Sure, you are so wooed. With help from my trusty bachelor pad."

"I think it's our bachelor pad," she replies sleepily.

"What does that even mean?"

"Love means not having to explain afterglow banter. Go back to sleep."

CHAPTER 47

As a long-standing ritual, John goes into the office on quiet Sunday afternoons to declutter his office in preparation for the upcoming week. This includes clean-up of both his voice and email mailboxes. While deletion of junk email is performed almost daily via his laptop, the voice mailbox is largely a relic of the old office phone system. In trying to reach the CEO without being screened, phone solicitors call in after hours and use the dial-by-name directory to find John's extension. The resulting mailbox contains ninety-nine-percent commercial solicitations, amid other audio detritus.

His left hand is dedicated to voicemail clean-up, with

the index finger hovering over the #1 key on the touchtone dial for message deletion as soon as the gist of it becomes clear. His right hand is for email with the index finger on the keyboard's delete key. John derives secret enjoyment pitting email and voicemail purges against one another, and now, he preps for the exciting multi-tasking race. Email deletion is usually the easy winner since it frequently requires only the briefest glance at the subject line:

-      Warning, your accounts may be breached... DELETE

-      Let Annuities Protect Your Retirement Income in 2023... DELETE

-      Electric Lighter Selling Like Hotcakes... DELETE

-      Tired of waiting for those blue pills... DELETE

By contrast, voice messages require about one second of listening before the left hand is approved to kill the message. But the left hand can build up a head of steam as voice messages abound:

"Hi, John. Are you looking to outsource your..." DELETE

"Did you know your window for claiming a settlement is still open..." DELETE

"Hi, John. My name is Carolyn Hertzinger. Have you ever considered franchising…" DELETE

After about five minutes, the email in-box is free of junk, but the voice backlog still flows freely:

"We have COVID tests for your company…" DELETE

"This is the warranty department. Your car's warranty has expired, leaving you…" DELETE

"Hello, John. This is Alec Cramer. I am…" John's left index finger is hovering over the #1 key. In that instant, something in John's memory causes the twitchy digit to freeze. Alec Cramer? The name rings a bell. He presses #2 instead to restart the message.

"Hello, John. This is Alec Cramer. I am CEO of Hundo. I have been hearing good things about Victech and am interested in buying your company. Please give me a call…"

John has heard of Hundo. Based in Palo Alto with satellite offices around the world, he knows that in recent years, the company has had explosive growth, becoming a sprawling tech conglomerate. They have rolled up acquisitions in data management, AI, and platform-building applications. Receiving an unsolicited call to discuss a possible buyout by a company of this stature is a rare event that most startups never experience. This is a company with the potential to create a lucrative exit for Victech, if both parties were to believe it is a good fit.

"Wow, we almost missed that!" he says aloud, apparently addressing his left index finger. No response from the chastened finger.

The timestamp on the message is Friday around 9:30 p.m. ET, which means Alec left it around 6:30 p.m. in Palo Alto. John will return the call tomorrow. That will give him ample time to do further research on the Hundo empire and Mr. Cramer.

CHAPTER 48

Publicly-held companies are required to provide an abundance of information not easily obtained from privately-held firms. Details on finances, major investors, sources of revenue among its divisions, and acquisitions paint a detailed picture of how the firm operates.

For large tech companies, like Hundo, a strategy of growth-by-acquisition can be especially attractive when flush with cash from a public offering. It takes a long time before companies become large enough to attract SEC scrutiny as potential monopoly suspects. There was a period in the early 1990s when Cisco was said to be completing a new acquisition every couple of weeks.

In less than five years since going public, Hundo Enterprises had grown its revenue to $1.3 Billion. During that time, they continued to accelerate their buying spree, seeking fresh technical innovations sprouting in their chosen markets.

Co-founder Alec Cramer is the CEO. His background includes early success in selling green screen technology to Wall Street. John quickly deduces Alec's interest in Victech lies in its penetration into the healthcare space, where Hundo currently has a minimal footprint.

Interestingly, John notes that while Hundo has a presence in numerous locations around the globe, there are few physical offices of any size. The use of shared office space and work from home were trends even before the pandemic. These operating models grew rapidly in popularity during mandated lockdowns. While Victech supported some level of work from home, both before and during the pandemic, the company reverted to a largely centralized business once it was deemed safe. Post-pandemic, many employees would continue to work from home but only once or twice a week. John believes having an organization too physically dispersed and scattered fails to create a binding, common culture. If talks between

Hundo and Victech should go anywhere, John would want further research on the cultural fit.

It is Monday and California is awake. The direct number Alec left in the voicemail permits John to connect after only a couple of rings.

"Hi, Alec. This is John Victor returning your call."

"Hello, John. Thanks for returning my call. Nice to make your acquaintance."

"Thanks, Alec. Delighted to meet you as well. I must say your message took me by surprise."

Alec laughs. "I like direct, to-the-point introductions. Preferably without intermediaries or screening. Do you know much about our company?"

"A bit. It is seen as well run by the Street. Impressively fast growth. Very strong in data management and platform-building. Also, highly acquisitive."

"Excellent, and thank you. Yes, we only enter markets where our advantages will enable us to become market leaders within a couple of years. Our acquisition strategy is to find companies that can act as booster rockets for us to enter a new space, based on a formidable technology lead. We believe Victech may fit that profile, given your presence in healthcare."

John nods to himself as Alec confirms his guess as to why he had interest in buying Victech. In the discussion that ensues, Alec asks John for details about Victech; its finances, ownership structure, and the size and composition of its customer base. John responds freely and openly to all questions. He knows it's best to enter this discussion in a pure sales mode. Asking for a non-disclosure agreement at this early of a stage is not worth the obstruction it could create or the opportunity it could squander. Despite the competitive breach once caused by the duplicity of Carl Redder, John realizes that more disclosure in this context carries greater upside opportunity than downside risk. He speaks boldly of the company's growth, unique market positioning, and momentum.

He is equally bold in asking Alec about the probable shape a merger might take; would an acquisition be paid out in cash vs. stock, would the Victech team be kept intact, what is the level of autonomy the Victech leadership team would have ongoing? Wherever possible, Alec is forthcoming with positive answers, including an all-cash offer if and when they get that far. One more advantage of a cash-rich public company, John thinks.

Both parties are pleased with the information received

in this first contact. They agree that the next interaction will involve a much deeper dive; requesting answers to dozens of written questions to be provided to Victech.

Before winding up the call, Alec mentions a caveat, "There is one thing I must advise you on up-front, John. There can be no disclosures about any discussions between our companies. If it becomes known that Hundo is in discussion with you, or if you should invite other companies in to competitively bid, any terms we may have proposed to you will be automatically withdrawn."

"Of course," John replies. "As long as we agree on a deadline by which the restriction is lifted if a transaction has not been completed."

"Perfect. Thank you, John. I have greatly enjoyed this exchange. Looking forward to taking the next steps."

CHAPTER 49

Lyra receives John's Slack invitation to meet for lunch today. It is two days earlier than their normal routine. Hunan Lion on a Tuesday instead of Thursday? Outrageous. Something must be up. Plus, it's a miserable travel day. Snow-covered roads are getting worse by the hour. She would have preferred working from home today using Slack and Zoom while secretly wearing comfy slippers. Regardless, she arrives at the restaurant and locates a quiet booth. John arrives shortly and joins her.

"I've ordered a fifty-gallon drum of hot and sour soup," she says.

"Sounds like a good starter. Are you familiar with

Hundo?" John asks, cutting to the chase.

"The Valley, right? Platform building tools. NASDAQ. Crazy growth."

"Yep, mostly through acquisitions. They want to buy us."

"OK, you now have my full attention."

During the next hour, as lunch is ordered, served, and consumed, John recounts the voice message and details from his subsequent phone exchange with Alec. Over orange shrimp and Kung Pao chicken, he debriefs Lyra on what he has gleaned about this multinational company from Sunday's research.

"So, they see us as a way to launch Hundo into healthcare? Makes sense."

"Speaking of 'launch,' he used the term 'booster rockets' to describe their acquisition targets."

"I don't love the metaphor. Most booster rockets are expendable."

"OK, let's assume he wasn't being literal."

"How serious do you think this is?"

"I have no reason to suspect otherwise at this point. If it were competitive reconnaissance, he wouldn't have placed the call personally. Chief Executive of a public company snooping around—not a good look. The direct call signals seriousness. But we are early in the dance; there are many steps left before we get a term sheet, should it go that far."

"Any hints on valuation?"

"Not yet. Probably a good time for us to update our research on recent comps. Marianne can help."

"What do we tell the team?"

"Good question. I don't want to distract everyone or have them asking a thousand questions before we have answers."

"Maybe just Marianne, Marcus, and Ernie for now?"

"Agreed. Plus, the outside Board members: Tim and Katy. It's important we all keep this close to the vest until we have a better sense if it's going anywhere. If it should, I suspect due diligence will be a beast. Marianne may have to deputize some admins to help us compile the package."

Lyra says, "You know the next question I must ask: how does our recent discussion about succession align with this new development?"

John thinks for a moment, "I'm not sure yet. I imagine a buyer would perceive having two leaders as a plus, in case the first proves flaky. And speaking of which, I don't believe you have declared your intentions."

"Correct, I have not." John can't read any hint from her response and Lyra's expression remains noncommittal. She presses ahead, "So, what is our next step with the Mighty Hundo?"

"They are asking us to respond and expound on a written list of questions they will provide."

"Bring it."

Their lunch has ended, so they stand and don their heavy, winter garb.

John adds, "FYI—I meant to mention, I'm pretty sure Lynn and Maddy are coming home to stay."

Lyra stops in her tracks and smiles warmly, "That's wonderful news, John. I'm so happy for you."

They head toward the door, seeing the weather outside worsening.

"Well, was the news worth traveling here on a miserable day like this?" John asks.

"If you mean the news of our corporate suitor, too early to say. Ask me again in a few months. But if you mean the news of you reuniting with your family—hell yes."

CHAPTER 50

"You can stop clenching, Mom. We're really OK," Maddy is driving her mother to Susan's house.

"You're doing fine, honey," Lynn responds. "What makes you think I'm clenching?"

"Well, there are your closed fists, the sucking sound you're making through your teeth, and your right foot attempting to push a non-existent brake pedal. All very incriminating stuff, Mom."

"Never mind that. Did Driver's Ed specifically cover winter driving?"

"Sure, they told us the roads are slippery, so get where we're going fast by driving like hell."

"Not funny, Maddy. Not funny."

Road conditions add an extra fifteen minutes to the drive time. When they finally arrive, Whitney welcomes them into the warm house. Susan and Maddy immediately disappear into Susan's bedroom, both yacking it up in incessant, rapid whispers.

Lynn and Whitney hug hello, fondly watching their daughters take off. Like their daughters, the two have recently grown closer as friends. Their girls provide the primary common bond. However, with their respective spouses both full time at Victech, there is always much to share.

They enter the kitchen and Whitney serves coffee and light snacks. Lynn asks, "How is Susan doing?"

"Much better than we expected—especially this early. You know she is a sweet and shy girl, but very loving. From what we were told before the adoption, we thought it could be months, or even years, before she came out of her shell. We expected her to be as fragile as a hothouse flower, but what is remarkable is how much she has opened up to Marcus and me."

"That's wonderful to hear, Whitney. I remember how introverted she was, even before all of this happened. Is she able to socialize with others okay?"

"Too early to tell. She trusts us, and she trusts Maddy, but still harbors a fear of strangers." Whitney sighs. "She's been damaged, Lynn. We honestly don't know how deep or long lasting."

"That must be so hard. I'm sorry. What you are doing for her is wonderful. You and Marcus are truly good people."

"Thank you, I appreciate that. Can I ask, did you know her mother?"

"Melinda? Not really. I met her once or twice. Most of what I know of her is not flattering, though. I don't believe for a second that she didn't know what that bastard was doing to her daughter. Horrible…" Lynn starts to tear up, recalling that terrifying night and the police's endless questioning of Maddy.

"It's OK, it doesn't matter now." Whitney puts her hand on Lynn's. "Susan is our daughter now, and she is safe."

Lynn smiles appreciatively and changes the subject. "I do have some good news to share."

"Well dish, lady!"

"Maddy and I are moving back home."

John and Lynn had shared only the basic facts about

their separation with a few close friends. Lynn had made some remarks to Whitney about John's excessive work week without detail, but like others, Marcus and Whitney had been largely left to speculate why in the world these two great people were not getting along. Of course, Lynn knew the open question of John stepping down from his position could not be disclosed to anyone at this stage, so her explanation is that John is willing to spend more time with his wife and daughter.

Whitney lights up. "That's sensational news! I am so happy for you! Maddy must be thrilled. So, when will you be leaving Marsha's smothering embrace?"

Lynn laughs aloud. "Very soon. Maybe next week. I've already plotted the breakout."

"Breakout? Sounds very Shawshank to me."

"Yeah, that's about right."

CHAPTER 51

John projects the questions on the conference room wall for the group to review. In attendance are Lyra, Marcus, Ernie, and Marianne.

"The code name is 'WCC' starting now. Stands for West Coast Company. I've put the initials of the primary respondent next to each question. As you can see, most of the questions belong to Marianne with a few for Lyra and Ernie. I've asked Marianne to be the overall editor, and all five of us will review the draft. Lyra and I will be the final proofing editors. No printed copies—we'll collaborate online using a private Slack channel."

"How long do we have?" Marianne asks.

"Fast and thorough speaks most strongly for our response. I'd like to respond to WCC by end-of-day today. That means, we need your initial drafts in the next couple of hours."

Ernie says, "How much detail do you want?"

"Responsive and succinct. The essentials you would want to know if you were the buyer. Work in sales points where you can, but don't ramble."

Everyone nods. As they leave the room, John Victor channels John Lennon, "I would like to say thank you on behalf of the group and ourselves, and I hope we pass the audition."

***

Ten minutes later, Lyra enters John's office. Upon seeing her, John says, "About our triple secret topic; we cannot be disclosing things to WCC we haven't announced internally."

"My thoughts exactly. It's a matter of trust. All the more reason it is fortunate that when I awoke this morning, I declared today to be my 'Yes Day'."

"'Yes Day'? Is that like 'Yesterday'?"

"Much better because it's today. It is a day of 'yes'."

John ponders this, "We are talking about succession, correct?"

"Yes."

"So, you are saying…?"

"Fuck yes!"

Lyra is beaming and John hugs her. Each is aware this decision marks a milestone.

They strategize on the announcement and its timing. In the written responses to Hundo, they will tee up the possibility of Lyra's future role but will not confirm the succession plan explicitly before the Team has been advised.

Lyra thinks to herself, the day of 'yes' has only just begun.

CHAPTER 52

Later that evening, Ed and Lyra are celebrating. "You did it, sweetie! You are the next CEO of Victech. Wow, just incredible!"

Dinner is over, and they are enjoying a Super Tuscan wine in the family room of Ed's house.

"It feels like the right move at the right time."

"You wavered for so long. What finally convinced you to make the leap?"

"Sometimes, it's just guts. I declared today to be my 'Yes Day'; a day of affirmative responses."

"So, you had planned to accept it today?"

"All affirmative responses, all day. Note the plural."

"OK, you had more than one "yes" in store?"

"Think long and hard, Eddie."

A pregnant pause. He stares at her.

"Ask me, Eddie."

"Don't mess with me. I can't tell if you're being serious."

"Ask me, Eddie."

"I don't want to be like Charlie Brown with the football."

"Just ask me, Eddie."

Ed rises swiftly from his chair and leaves the room. He quickly returns bearing a very small box. He walks over to her on the couch. She stands. He drops to one knee before her and presents the ring. "Will you marry me, Lyra Keller?"

"Fuck yes, I will, Eddie!"

He stands to his feet, taking her into his arms. They embrace, kiss, then embrace even tighter.

"I am so very, very happy," Ed says. "I love you."

"Back 'atcha," she responds. Then a whisper, "I love you, Eddie."

CHAPTER 53

Victech's Board convenes a special in-person session in the second week of the new year. John, Lyra, and Marianne join Katy and Tim in the latter's legal office downtown. Lyra will assume her new role as the company's Chief Executive on June first, as per unanimous vote of the Board two days earlier. The announcement was made to the full company at yesterday's team meeting. Tim and Katy now offer their in-person congratulations to Lyra.

Katy, known for her active support and promotion of women executives, is especially strong in her praise of the decision. Lyra's admiration for Katy is mutual. "It's wonderful. You are an inspiration and a role model for girls and women."

"Thank you, Katy. Coming from you, I cannot tell you how much that means to me."

Lyra has chosen to withhold news of her engagement for now. Even from John. Too many plates spinning at the moment, she had explained to Ed. He agreed to defer telling friends and family for now as well.

After everyone has been able to give Lyra their congratulations, John starts the meeting. Following a brief review of the financials by Marianne, they quickly move on to the main course: reviewing the status of the WCC negotiations.

John expounds on the recent events, "As you know, our response to their submitted questions was favorably received. This was acknowledged first in an email to me from Matt Penvoy and soon by a direct phone call from him. Matt introduced himself as V.P. of Corporate Development at WCC. Clearly, he is the appointed front man for negotiations. The initial call was a series of follow-up questions, mostly requesting elaboration of our written responses."

Katy asks, "Did you disclose Lyra's new role?"

"We decided to be a bit coy in the written responses,"

Lyra explains. "We had not yet informed the team."

"Matt did push on that a bit in the phone call, though," John continues. "He asked about the scope of Lyra's role. I told him to consider her as a co-CEO for all practical purposes."

"So much for subtlety," Lyra says.

"At the end of our first call, Matt scheduled a one-on-one Zoom for us for this past Monday. In that session, he started pontificating about valuations. He made some general observations about our revenue and market position. He suggested our focus on insurers would make for a somewhat indirect entry into healthcare. It wasn't exactly criticism but it was clearly intended to soften us up for what came next. He then floated that he feels a fair valuation for Victech would likely be in the $35-$45 million range."

There are glances around the room. After a moment, Katy asks, "What do you think of that, John?"

"It's a trial balloon. I did not react, but personally, I think it's a lowball."

Tim says, "What's the next step?"

"Matt set a marker, and we need to respond in kind. We will draft a gracious and friendly letter making the case for a higher number."

Katy asks, "What do you think our ask should be?"

"I think we can build a credible case for a market value of maybe $80-$90 million. We can buttress it with revenue multiples from comparable transactions."

Marianne, visibly both stimulated and frightened says, "What if we overshoot so much they walk away?"

"The risk is small if it's done right. Not adamant, just blue skying our thoughts like Matt did. You know, two guys talking. But even so, we'll have many strong points in our favor."

Lyra adds, "Including top customer names, a large serviceable market, a dramatic sales ramp and proof we are light-years ahead of competition."

John polls each Director in turn for their opinions and sees they are all excited for the most part. Tim and Marianne express concern about the risk but agree a well-produced letter is the best way to respond. Lyra is pumped and anxious for the opportunity to sell their value to WCC.

Katy's assessment is both candid and comprehensive in summarizing the Board's stance: "I am thrilled the company has reached this point. I am both excited and… yes… slightly apprehensive about what happens next. But my confidence in the three of you and the Victech team has never been stronger. Suffice to say, go write the world's best counter-offer!"

CHAPTER 54

John composes the response as a personal letter to
Matt. It begins with John's sincere thanks to Alec Cramer
and Matt for their consideration of Victech and their
straight forward approach to these discussions. He praises
Hundo's excellent performance and reputation, and with
phrasing help provided by Lyra, John notes that, although
far smaller than Hundo, he has always considered Victech
to be of the same breed of long-distance winners in Tech.

Next, he recaps the key selling points about the Victech
product line, the company's unique market positioning,
prestigious customer base, and their competitive
dominance. It cites the large Aerie deal as an example of

Victech's extraordinary credentials.

Toward the end, he thanks Matt again for sharing his preliminary thoughts about valuation and offers to return the favor in this letter. Marianne has provided an impressive hand-picked list of M&A transactions by companies in the Healthcare IT market space, including their mean and median multiples of their most recent twelve-month revenue at time of their acquisition. John uses those multiples to project their own valuation for Victech. He also provides a second approach by focusing on Victech's operating margins which are consistently high. Last year, they were twenty-five percent, which John politely notes are roughly double those of Hundo. Using these approaches with current revenue, John suggests a valuation potentially in the $85-$95 million range.

The letter next provides ten bullet points explaining why Victech should be viewed as a "top quartile" company, which is a concept often used by consultancies to rank tech companies. John recaps the acceleration potential of selling Victech technology through the Hundo's network. He includes a succinct recap of the company's mentoring and diversity programs, supplied by Marcus, and notes the recognition the company has received as being among the best places to work in Central Ohio.

In concluding the letter, John states that the correct valuation must be fair and rational for both parties and expresses hope that John and Matt can find common ground. John offers a face-to-face meeting if desired, either in Palo Alto or Columbus.

After re-reading his response a half-dozen times, he sends it.

That evening, he tells Lynn they should expect either a counter-offer or a fuck-you.

***

The call to John's cell comes just after 6:30 a.m. PT. John reads between the lines that the early call suggests a sense of urgency by Matt.

"Good morning, Matt."

"Hi, John. How are you doing?"

"I'm fine, thanks. I assume you received our letter?"

"Yes, and we have taken our time perusing it. It is very well composed, and you make some excellent points, a few we actually agree with, but others, not so much."

"Thanks Matt. Much appreciated," John says, ignoring

the mixed review.

"I want to be direct, John. Hundo cannot take the risk of overpaying for an acquisition, even one of this relatively modest size. We think Victech is a solid and growing company, with a strong management team, but we must keep in mind there's the risk that it may not take us into the Healthcare industry as fully as we hope…"

John is aware Matt's next words will tell him where all of this is going.

"Because of that, we cannot see the full consideration for Victech exceeding sixty, no matter how many comps you provide."

Without hesitation, John sets the hook, "Well Matt, we appreciate your candor. However, I can assure you the Victech Board will not approve an offer of less than sixty."

"OK, let me report this discussion back to our Corporate Development team and get back to you."

"Very good, Matt. Looking forward to the next steps."

The offer was, of course, already prepared and awaiting only insertion of the agreed upon figure. It arrived within the next two hours. It came in the form of a letter from Matt, including a two-page term sheet formalizing the $60 million offer.

In a hastily arranged Zoom call, the Victech's Board reacts with excitement. John describes the next steps, which feature his and Lyra's trip to Palo Alto to meet the principals and responding to the due diligence requests, which cover more than one hundred categories of Victech documentation.

Within the Board, the increase in valuation from the prior figure also gives rise to a shift in the greed-versus-fear calculus. Following John's update, Tim tests John's sense of the valuation. "I'm starting to wonder if perhaps we should continue pursuing the $80-$90 million valuation you made the case for in the letter. It was clearly persuasive."

John nips it in the bud, "It's not going to happen. Matt drew a hard line at sixty. It is the best and final. I would remind you all of the uncertainty this Board expressed just days ago that we could improve the original figure at all. Well, we've bumped it fifty-percent. My recommendation, let's take the win and press on." They all nod in agreement, including Tim. John continues, "It's too early to pop the champagne, as we literally owe them thousands of pages of due diligence response, but I'm optimistic. We just need to be realistic that there are plenty of opportunities for this thing to derail. We cannot be complacent."

"How long do you expect the diligence to take?" Marianne asks.

"At least a week is my current guess. Drafting of the formal deal can proceed in parallel."

"Very exciting stuff," Katy says. "Let's make it happen!"

CHAPTER 55

Due diligence is the mainstay process of successful mergers and acquisitions. It is the buyer's most thorough screen for finding hidden flaws or other surprises. As exemplified by past wreckages, such as Theranos, relying on hype, public perception, or earlier investors in lieu of full due diligence is a recipe for disaster.

The list provided by Hundo includes each and every contract, license agreement, employment agreement, Board minutes, legal actions, compensation details, policies & procedures, product plans, financial reports, and other documentation going back to its founding. The process hoovers up every important document ever produced within the company. For a company like Victech, with an almost twenty-year history, finding and reproducing a thorough set of digital documents is a massive undertaking.

To manage the review process, Victech utilizes a Virtual Data Room, which controls access to the confidential documents to minimize the risk of exposure to third parties. Granting, restricting, and revoking access on a per document type per reader basis is controlled by a senior Victech IT manager, assigned to Marianne for the duration of the due diligence. Depending on the document type, permission levels are set for different users and groups, from view-only to copy-and-print.

Marianne has also assigned members of the admin staff to help her, in addition to several temp workers. Because it is still premature to notify the team of the Letter of Intent and in-process negotiations, all staff members brought in on this project are sworn to secrecy. The management team has been advised only that John and Lyra will meet with a west coast firm that has expressed interest in exploratory talks with Victech.

Merger discussions inflict a high cost on small and midsized companies in terms of management distraction, company diversion, and the risk of false expectations. In addition to answering specific questions, John and Lyra hope the visit will allow them to further gauge Hundo's intentions and paint a more complete picture of what life will look like should the acquisition actually occur.

CHAPTER 56

Vaso is a rooftop bar located in the AC hotel in Dublin, Ohio. It rises over Dublin's popular Bridge Park community, proffering grand views of the city. On this evening, Whitney has persuaded Lynn to join her for a girls' night out, featuring tapas and drinks. Lynn has ordered a Mojito while Whitney enjoys an Expresso Martini. Whitney introduces Lynn to her young friend, Nicole.

Facing Whitney, Nicole says, "I am, like, so amazed you are here." Then turning to Lynn, "I have only been trying to get Whitney to come out with me for a drink for, like, a year. How did you pull this off?"

"The stars aligned tonight," Whitney says. "Lynn's daughter is sleeping over with Susan, and Marcus has graciously volunteered for chaperone duty."

"And my husband is in California on business," Lynn adds. "So, for once, Whitney and I are free to play."

She and Whitney clink their glasses, and Nicole joins the toast with a Blue Hawaiian. After a few minutes of small talk and icebreakers, Lynn learns that Whitney knows Nicole and her parents from their church. Lynn finds the girl engaging but also, apparently, distracted by all the young men entering the bar, so she asks Nicole if she has a boyfriend.

"Not currently," Nicole says.

"Nicole recently broke up with Mr. Wrong. Maybe this is a good spot to meet someone, Nicole. Don't let us cramp your style," Whitney says, winking at her.

"I've never been here before. It's a bit too pricey for my friends," Nicole responds. "As far as boyfriends, I'm honestly in no hurry to find a new one. There's more to life—like finding a decent job. Did you guys both have boyfriends when you were my age? I'm twenty-five."

"Let's see. At twenty-five, I was pregnant with Maddy," Lynn says.

"I was already a mother," Whitney adds. "But it doesn't matter. It's not a race, honey. You're smart, very pretty, and you've got plenty of time."

More drinks arrive at the table, and the discussion turns into Lynn and Whitney providing unsolicited dating advice for Nicole. Before long, it devolves further as the three share hyperbolic tales of the worst dates they ever had. Between drinks, Lynn and Whitney find themselves competing for the raunchiest bad date story. Uproarious laughter soon emanates from their table, catching the attention and some glares of other guests seated nearby.

After another ten minutes of Lynn and Whitney holding court, Nicole politely announces she sees someone she knows at the other side of the bar. She graciously thanks her hosts for the fun evening, excuses herself, and staggers away.

"Too rough for her?" Whitney asks.

"We had to cut her free," Lynn says.

"Fly little one!" Whitney flaps her arms.

"Caw, caw!" Lynn shrieks. Both laugh hysterically until their sides ache. When the laughter subsides, Lynn confesses feeling more than a little buzzed from the Mojitos.

Over the next half hour, they order coffee and return to talk about their families and the future. "How does Marcus feel about Lyra taking the reins next June?"

"He has the greatest respect for Lyra, and he's always been tight with her. At the same time, he wonders how much interaction he'll still have with John day-to-day."

"Not sure in terms of Victech, but you know our families' friendship will only grow."

They clink coffee mugs.

"So, what exactly is John doing out in California?"

"Silicon Valley stuff. You know, he and Lyra are rubbing elbows with the big boys!" Lynn says, intending to be funny. She immediately regrets it as she sees a shadow cross Whitney's face.

"Is there a merger on the table?" Whitney asks suddenly. Her directness shocks Lynn.

"Whit—I don't know. I can't say. If there were, would that be a problem?"

"It could be. Before Victech, Marcus had been H.R. Director for five years when his previous employer was acquired and he was laid off. That's when he started doing freelance work. We had no income stability. Acquisitive companies usually have their own H.R. departments, which makes Marcus' role an easy target for headcount reduction."

Lynn is upset with herself for putting her foot in her mouth; she didn't mean to take their fun banter down this rat hole. "John values Marcus enormously. He would not let that happen!"

Whitney puts her hand on Lynn's and responds soberly, "It may not be John's decision."

CHAPTER 57

John and Lyra reach the Hundo campus late Monday afternoon Pacific Time. Matt Penvoy greets them in the lobby of the main HQ building and ushers them into a conference room. They are introduced to executives representing North America Sales, Marketing, Finance, and Product Development. All carry a title reflecting some sort of V.P., Senior or Executive, or else Chief Something Officer. Business cards fly around the table.

After the initial intros, Matt opens the discussion for Q&A.

Winston, the Sales Chief, directs questions to John primarily about Victech's market size, demographics, and penetration. John defers most questions to Lyra, adding his own color commentary where appropriate. He directly responds to financial questions from Jean, the Finance Chief.

In order for it to not feel entirely like an inquisition, Lyra and John are also permitted to pose questions to their hosts. They inquire about the size of the campus, how regions are structured, and how personnel are distributed around the world. They also ask what level of autonomy individual divisions hold. The reporting structure strikes them as somewhat garbled and, apparently, variable by division and location.

After about an hour, Matt announces there are special dinner plans for the guests and gives them time to check in to their hotel rooms before dinner. He advises them that Hundo CEO Alec Cramer will be attending the dinner in Menlo Park and looks forward to meeting them in person.

On their way back to the rental car, Lyra says to John, "Let the games begin."

CHAPTER 58

Monday night's dinner turns out to be a sublime affair. The next morning, John and Lyra are still reliving it in the car returning to the Hundo campus. "Of course, the venue had to be Sand Hill Road in Menlo," John says. "Only home to the top V.C. firms. Kleiner, Andreessen, and Sequoia amongst them. And fine dining to boot. It was amazing."

"That restaurant, Madera, right? Was awesome. Definitely befits the upscale location. Not just the food. Did you notice the cars parked around the entrance?"

"I spotted a McClaren, a Bugatti, and a couple Rolls. I assume it's no-parking for anything under half a mill."

"Definitely not a good spot for your garden variety fender bender."

John and Lyra agree if the goal was to impress them, Alec had succeeded. He is a gracious host. The group included Matt, Winston, and Jean, among other executives, and the talk had been convivial and free of probing merger questions. Those are apparently queued for today's meetings, John thinks.

***

Upon their arrival, Matt gives John and Lyra a brief tour of the Hundo campus. The main building houses the CEO and his support group, Legal, and part of the Finance team. All other groups are in three larger buildings, separated by a well-manicured landscape and numerous walkways. The tree-lined paths contain ample greenspace and are complete with park benches. Open areas include a basketball court and an adjoining area for frisbee golf.

Matt informs them there are approximately 1800 employees in the Palo Alto location which comprises roughly twenty percent of Hundo's world-wide employment. Subsidized cafeterias in each building offer a wide selection of popular food types and provide an incentive for employees not to leave the campus for lunch. Large tech companies assume too much time away from campus is lost productivity.

Just before 10:00 a.m., Matt announces that Alec has requested a meeting with John and that Winston would like to meet concurrently with Lyra.

As they walk, Lyra whispers to John, "Divide and conquer?"

"Apparently. Maybe they feel outnumbered."

John is escorted to Alec's executive office. The room is sprawling and includes a conference table and a small sitting area. Alec waves John into a seat next to him. Several walls are lined with sports memorabilia alongside reprinted articles with covers featuring Alec and Hundo. Mounted in glass over the chairs is a jersey bearing the Hundo logo that catches John's attention.

"Hundo has its own cycling team," Alec explains. "Two, really, in the Palo Alto area. Our female team has been killing it this year. Are you a cyclist, John?"

"Not a racer. Back home I like to do thirty-to-sixty-mile rides with friends when time permits."

"Excellent. Is Ohio good for cycling?"

"It is. In Columbus, you only need to travel a half hour or less in any direction to find great country roads. Hundreds of miles of them, actually."

The friendly chat continues several minutes longer until Alec indicates a desire to change the subject. "I did want to ask you about Lyra. She makes a great impression. When we first contacted you, she was not particularly on our radar. But from your responses, Matt believes she is functioning more as a Co-CEO than a Sales & Marketing exec. Is that correct?"

"Indeed. We just announced internally she will be succeeding me as Chief Executive on June first. It has been in the works for some time, before you had contacted me even. Your written questions coincided with our securing Board approval."

"I see. And what do you see your role being after the first of June?"

"I plan to remain on, in an operational role and continue to backstop Lyra as needed. But as CEO, the plan is for her to be the final authority for all operational and strategic Victech decisions." John sees that Alec looks fretful and asks, "Do you foresee a problem?"

"Candidly, I'm not sure. Part of what we think we

would be acquiring with Victech is a team with a strong track record. Now, it seems as if a winning team is losing its top player."

"Let me put you at ease, Alec. Lyra joined us twelve years ago as our first Marketing Director. We were still a tiny company in 2011. From the start, she was instrumental to our growth. In 2021, she took over Sales, which had been struggling in the pandemic economy. She restructured and upgraded the entire department ground up. Under her leadership, it grew into the winning model we have today. She has mastered every part of our business and is greatly respected both internally and by our customers. She is also a Board member and has been effectively running Victech the last couple of years. She is not new to any of her responsibilities. I have no plans to go away, but even if I were taken out by a runaway bus tomorrow, Victech wouldn't lose a beat."

"OK, John. Thank you for the strong testimonial. I look forward to debriefing my senior team on their impressions."

"I appreciate you asking the direct question. Anything else I can weigh in on?"

"Well, yes. We're interested in learning more about a

most unusual agreement your company struck with a venture investment firm called RashCap."

John smiles. "Make yourself comfortable, Alec. This may take more than a few minutes."

CHAPTER 59

Aboard the evening return flight from San Jose to Columbus, John and Lyra find a chance to further share details of their respective meetings. But first, he hands her a soft gray plastic bag. From it, she removes an article of clothing festooned with commercial logos. Foremost among them is the bold Hundo imprimatur.

"What is this?"

"A parting gift from Alec. It's a cycling jersey for Team Hundo. They gave me one too. We have been anointed honorary members of their cycling team."

Lyra looks aghast. "Is yours pink like mine?"

"No. Mine is blue, of course."

"Too bad," she says, holding the jersey alongside John's face. "Pink becomes you."

She studies the garment further. "The word 'garish' doesn't begin to cut it."

"Garish is de rigueur in the world of bike jerseys. Don't worry, I thanked him for the both of us."

Lyra rolls her eyes and changes the subject to one of greater interest. "About our separate meetings; I presume the topic of my ascendancy came up?"

"Indeed. Because we hadn't informed them of succession plans in our written responses, it raised some eyebrows. I spent some time replaying your Victech history and singing your praises. I assured Alec the company would have no problem carrying on with you at the helm if something were to happen to me. I think it stuck. How did it go with Winston?"

"It also went quite well. I described my vision of creating a high caliber sales team. He is a sales guy, and sales guys love to be sold. I think we are in sync."

"I agree. If not, we'll find out soon enough."

"What we didn't discuss yet are any staffing changes Hundo may require. Did you get anything on that?"

"A little," John says. "Because we have a couple

hundred employees, we qualify for having 'critical mass' in their eyes. That suggests they are unlikely to reassign our team members to begin reporting to Hundo managers outside of Victech. I believe that will apply to Sales, Support, and Product Development, at least for anytime in the near future. The two areas I am most concerned about them tampering with are Finance and H.R."

"Marianne and Marcus. Why them?"

"As a division, Victech will likely not need to produce its own financials. All of that will be rolled up into corporate. Marianne's staff will likely still do invoicing locally, but we have no detail on how that will work. Likewise, we don't know enough yet about their approach to Human Resources. It's usually quite different in a large corporation."

"Can we open discussions with Hundo corporate on these issues?"

"We need to hold off until the diligence and merger draft documents are in the final stages. The further along we get, the less likely that either party will allow one issue to derail the deal. Until then, this is all speculation."

They sit in silence for a few minutes. Then, Lyra turns to John as if she just remembered something from her to-do list. "By the way," she says, "I forgot to mention this earlier; I'm engaged."

John stares blankly at her for a moment before saying, "Congratulations to you and Ed. Was this another part of your 'Yes Day'?"

She nods, impressed he made the connection. "It was a great day. It just happened, so we haven't set a date yet or anything."

"It's never a dull moment with you, is it?"

"I certainly hope not."

CHAPTER 60

Mergers and acquisitions are a legal specialty. Victech has retained Columbus-based Kenny Gandolfo, also known as K.G., to represent them in merger discussions based on Tim's recommendation. John did not expect Hundo to use in-house counsel to negotiate the transaction, but he was surprised to learn they also did not use a California-based law firm. Rather, they retained a prestigious New York firm, McKillen Associates. John concluded the N.Y. lawyers must be more cutthroat than their west coast brethren. Certainly, no less expensive.

The internal kickoff meeting includes K.G., Marianne, and Lyra. In person, K.G. presents John with a printed version summarizing the main merger document he has received from McKillen. John is horrified by its size.

"The term sheet is only two pages," John exclaims. "How can that spawn this behemoth?" He thumbs through it in wonder. "This puppy weighs in at almost two hundred fun-filled pages."

K.G. explains the first draft contains mostly boilerplate templates and that the superfluous sections will be rescinded, or at least reduced, as they work through it. He describes his approach to the negotiation, saying that in two days, he will have reviewed the document and marked it up with his notes and changes. K.G. will then send them to John for review with whomever John needs to pull in from Victech. Then John and K.G. will collaborate on open issues by phone, making any necessary further adjustments. The marked-up copy will be returned to McKillen as the first official revision. McKillen will then create the second revision, conferring with K.G. as needed, to resolve open issues. Rinse and Repeat.

"We do, however, have an early issue to address," K.G. adds. "McKillen has advised us there is a question of sales tax liability with your licensed customers."

"That makes no sense," says Marianne. "Our licenses

explicitly hold the customer responsible for all sales and use taxes."

K.G. says, "They did not elaborate, but suggested we convene a conference call with both parties and their respective counsels to address the issue."

John shrugs. "Fine. I don't really understand what the issue is, K.G., but go ahead and set it up for us. Schedule it for first thing tomorrow, as soon as the west coast wakes up."

***

K.G. initiates the conference call with John, Marianne, and Lyra. The three are together in the Victech conference room. Matt joins the call from Palo Alto, along with Stuart, a McKillen lawyer calling in from New York. After being introduced to the group, Stuart leads the discussion. "We are reviewing hundreds of Victech customer agreements. Apparently, the standard license template requires the licensee to pay all sales and use taxes, but does your company confirm that these taxes are actually paid?"

"We don't audit customers sales tax payments, no," Marianne explains.

"So, you don't know whether the tax is paid or not. We believe that represents a potential liability," Stuart says.

With her palms up, Lyra silently mouths the words, 'What the Fuck'?

John steps in, "It is an obligation of the licensee, Stuart. In what sense is it a liability of ours?"

"Tax authorities can come after you. If you learn that one of your best customers has not paid the tax, are you really going to demand they do so?"

"Fuck yes! In a heartbeat," Lyra says—aloud this time.

There is a brief silence on the call before Matt jumps in and tries another approach, "John, what if we were to lower the total consideration, perhaps by a couple million as an insurance reserve against future tax claims?"

"The Board has blessed this transaction at sixty," John calmly states.

"Suppose we were to agree to fifty-nine?" Matt asks. "What amount do you think would be fair as a set-aside for unpaid taxes?"

"Frankly, the answer is zero. I don't want to tinker with the consideration, Matt. With our customer base, we're talking about Fortune companies here. These are organizations with large legal and accounting groups. They know what they signed and which taxes they owe. None of them will fail to pay their sales taxes," John says, unwavering.

"OK," says Matt. "Let us take this under advisement within Hundo."

After the call has ended, K.G. texts John affirming he will press on with negotiations while awaiting Hundo's response.

"John, you know we've never had an issue with customers not paying sales tax," Marianne says. The three remain in the Victech conference room.

"This is ridiculous," Lyra says.

"Lawyers are paid to see potential problems, including ones that don't exist in real life," John says. "I think Matt is receptive to our thinking. This is a non-issue. He doesn't want this to be a deal-killer any more than we do. My bet is they'll ask for an extended escrow as a fallback. By the way, this won't be the last obstacle we'll encounter in this deal."

"That's good because we definitely need more drama in our lives," Lyra says.

CHAPTER 61

It is not long before John's predictions are proven correct. Driving home the same day, K.G. calls his cell. "Good news and bad news, John."

"My favorite opening line. Hit me."

"The good news is there is no change in the total consideration. They do want to bump the escrow up to twenty-five-percent, though, and extend it for eighteen months. That gives them time to research and determine how much sales tax exposure they may really have."

"Fine. Eighteen months is the absolute limit."

"They also plan to have someone individually contact all major customers to verify there is no unpaid tax."

"Swell. As long as Sales blesses their script so we're not embarrassed, they can knock themselves out. Anything else?"

"The bad news part; the Victech 2016 stock option plan is void."

"What are you talking about?"

"It was never approved by the stockholders."

"Sure, it was. The vote is recorded in the Board minutes. You should have a copy."

"It required a vote by a majority of stockholders."

"Back then, the Board included me and all the V.C.s. Easily a majority at that time."

"But you were all voting in your capacity as Directors, not shareholders."

"It's the same fucking group of people!"

"Doesn't matter. If you had adjourned the Board meeting and then called for them to vote as shareholders, it would be legit. As it is, all grants made under that plan are void. I guess the good news is, the company doesn't owe a cent for any of those grants."

John is fuming. Grants made under the original stock option plan went to early key people like Lyra, Marcus, and Marianne. Those had long since vested. But the bulk of employee grants were issued under the revised 2016 plan and were intended to benefit the majority of employees during the company's most formidable growth years.

"Kenny, listen to me. We are going to directly compensate all employees identically to what they would have received had the 2016 plan been correctly approved. OK?"

"Sure. You can do that."

"Every last goddamn dime."

CHAPTER 62

Ever since Lynn and Maddy moved back home, John has done his best to be with them in the early evenings and immerse himself in family life without distractions.

John and K.G. have established a daily call routine to discuss the latest changes to the merger agreement from the Hundo legal team. It turns out, K.G. is an early riser, so John leaves the house by 6:30 a.m. and the two connect around 7:00 a.m. for their morning call. They review the open issues, making decisions on where concessions can and cannot be made. As merger negotiations progress, John tries not to drown Lynn by sharing the minutia of newly discovered obstacles, which he knows would stress her out.

No longer a full-time chauffeur for her newly-mobile daughter, Lynn's productivity has increased and her travel business continues to pick up. Her days are busy but also more relaxed. Maddy wants to start looking at college campuses, and John and Lynn suggest she start local, perhaps OSU or Otterbein. However, there is a new boy named Gary in Maddy's class who's looking at Purdue, so Maddy also wants to check out that school. She likes him a lot, and they have been studying together several evenings a week at Gary's house. When John asks whatever happened to Fredrick, Lynn rolls her eyes and Maddy replies, "Dad, that was like a million years ago. You really need to keep up."

Nevertheless, John and Lynn enjoy their extra alone time in the evenings, resulting from her study dates with Gary. Tonight, they start streaming a movie but pause it shortly after, as they drift into discussions about their future.

"You know if this thing closes, we'll be coming into more money than we've ever had," John says. "You had mentioned that your parents' house needs major work. We can certainly help them."

"Can we buy them a BMW too?" Lynn asks wryly.

"They need to replace Marsha's old Junker."

"Do they? Or are you trying to make a point to your mother?"

"Maybe both," she laughs. "But tell me, how are you feeling about all of this? I know wealth has never been your main driver. What will you tell young entrepreneurs that want to do what you have done?"

"I believe no rational person should undertake a twenty-year journey, like Victech, just for the possibility of an eventual payoff. Many entrepreneurs start off thinking it's the path to wealth, but unless they really relish the ride, it's too risky and difficult. For the bulk of startups, other than the rare exploder, wealth alone doesn't provide enough juice to go the distance. The odds are too long and so is the road."

"Let's talk about the Victor family's road. What's next?"

"I've already advised Hundo that you and I are scheduled to take a long-awaited vacation. I will take a month off and we'll do some traveling, so that comes first, regardless. If the deal closes, I'm with Hundo for at least eighteen months after that, which will mark the end of the escrow payments. Then, we're ready for a new chapter. Maddy will be off to college. You and I can travel to places we've never had the time or money to explore. I don't know how long Hundo will want to keep me around after the eighteen months, but I promise to never get so lost in my work again. Lyra is a strong leader—more so every day. As they see her in action, their comfort level in kissing me goodbye will increase. Of course, if they should open up some sort of interesting experience for me, I could stick around. Maybe. We'll just have to see."

"What if they want you to become the Hundo CEO someday?"

John laughs, "A giant public company? No thanks. Alec is welcome to it. I stopped being a corporate climber when I left Aurelian. That was twenty years ago. I found the startup world more exciting. Owning all the risk and reward. Exhilarating and terrifying of course, but always exciting."

"But this merger is really happening, isn't it? I mean, neither of us will ever need to work again if we don't want to, right? I can't quite wrap my head around it."

"Hang on, babe. We're almost at the finish line."

CHAPTER 63

John's letter, dated January 26, 2023, was sent out to all Victech shareholders almost nineteen years from the day the company was founded. It announced the letter of intent that has been signed with Hundo Enterprises and also that a merger agreement has been negotiated and unanimously approved by the Victech Board. It describes the share price and basic escrow provisions. Attached to the letter is the official Transaction Information Statement with accompanying exhibits. The letter calls for the prompt return of the shareholders' approval votes to be sent to the offices of Kenny Gandolfo, Esq.

The following Tuesday is the final senior staff meeting

before the merger. Lyra and John spend over an hour fielding questions about what life will look like after the acquisition.

"Hundo wants the merger agreement to take effect this month, which means it must be signed by midnight tonight," she explains. "We don't expect many changes in reporting relationships, but frankly, Hundo does not yet have these answers. We do know John and I will report into corporate."

Ernie goads Lyra, "You can't be called CEO anymore. What will your title be?"

"Officially, it will be Managing Director of the Victech Division. But you can still refer to me as Supreme Goddess as you always have, Ernie."

There are chuckles from the room.

"What's the status of the vote?" Marcus asks.

John responds, "Securing shareholder approval is the final step in completing the merger. Apparently, we have an issue with some of the lawyers from the old Jeffries group. Many of them actually do not recall they are investors in Victech and have an issue about approving the deal. I'm awaiting a call to learn more about that soon."

"Does the merger affect my timing at closing out the

year?" Marianne asks.

"Don't see why it would. Let's work under the assumption that nothing changes until we learn otherwise," Lyra says.

A staffer enters the room and announces that K.G. is on the phone for John. He leaves the meeting to take the call.

Lyra fields a few more questions before she ends the meeting. She asks Marianne and Marcus to stay over. With the room cleared, she addresses them together, "John and I have concerns about your respective positions in particular, so we put our questions directly to corporate. As expected, there are no firm commitments, but we did get some encouraging feedback. The last two acquisitions Hundo made of comparable size retained their fulltime CFO, which we think is promising for you, Marianne. I cannot tell you precisely how your job may change, we'll have to see. They alluded to the possibility of adding one or more of their smaller acquisitions into the Victech financials in some sort of roll-up, which you would presumably manage.

"On the H.R. front, Marcus, we learned some interesting things. There is no well-defined H.R. team in

Corporate. It's sort of handled by Legal, but not well. Alec recognizes the need to address this, and the company is contemplating creating a common set of policies to be used by an internal network of regional H.R. directors internationally. We took the liberty of sending them a copy of the Victech policy manual, authored by one Marcus Mitchell, and it has garnered a positive response. It sounds promising, but that's all we know so far."

Marcus replies first, "Lyra, this means a lot to me. Whether or not it works out, I greatly appreciate your efforts on my behalf. Thank you."

Marianne jumps in, "Same. We're here for the duration and beyond if they want us."

Lyra smiles warmly, thinking, but if they do not, I'm relieved that we verified you each have a boatload of vested stock options.

CHAPTER 64

John picks up the call, "K.G., what have we got?"

"There were twenty-five lawyers in the original Jeffries group that elected your 'half and half' put option twelve years ago. All except ten of them have agreed to the merger. We need most of those to reach our approval threshold of ninety-five-percent of total shares."

"What's the issue with the ten?"

"Most don't remember the investment. They fear incurring personal liability in case the transaction would turn out to be fraudulent."

"Really? Suggesting we committed fraud?"

"Yes. They said you're probably a great guy. They just

don't know you, and they think there's legal exposure if they approve the transaction. I was not able to dissuade them."

"Nice to know it isn't personal. Lawyers! What the hell is wrong with your ilk? And what do we do?"

"Here's my idea, you buy their shares personally. It removes them from the transaction entirely."

"Love it. What's the downside?"

"I suppose it means you'll theoretically be assuming even greater risk for the fraud scenario they fear."

John laughs, "If I had committed fraud, the additional risk from their shares would be a rounding error!"

"True. I recommend we buy them out for maybe eighty cents on the dollar. That's the cost of our insulating them from their perceived risk. It's insurance."

"OK. I think of it as sort of a fine for them being wimps. It's a great solution, K.G. Let's do it. Is this our last issue?"

"One more. This just popped up within the hour. You may recall Gohio Bank took some Victech warrants as part of your loan deal. They told me they would approve the transaction, but apparently, changed their mind after review by their legal team. I know—lawyers. No need to slam my ilk again."

"Same solution, right? I buy the shares?"

"Yes, but their last-minute flip-flop really pisses me off. I suggest we offer them sixty-five cents on the dollar."

"Done."

"Can you and Lyra swing by my office around 5 p.m. tonight? I have about a million documents for the two of you to sign to finalize the merger."

"Will do. I appreciate your creative solution. Nice work, K.G."

CHAPTER 65

Celebration at the Victor household takes the form of Carlucci's Pizza and wine for the adults. After inhaling two slices, Maddy announces she is going over to Gary's house to study.

Lynn calls her bluff, "Finals week is over. What exactly are you two studying now?"

"College planning stuff. Also, we listen to music sometimes."

John says, "If it's music you want, this is the place to be. Your friendly Musicologist father has a special show planned for you. Tonight, we will cover those songs, which includes the line, 'let your backbone slip.' Fun, huh?"

"Yuck. What does that even mean?"

"I suspect it was a sixties euphemism for shake your ass," John says. "It predates twerking."

"Weird. No thanks. I'll be back by ten. Bye-bye." Maddy grabs her coat and bolts out the door.

"That was an impressively fast getaway," John notes. He turns to Lynn. "Let your backbone slip?"

"No thanks. At our age, we'd need to call a chiropractor."

John pours them each another glass of wine. They sit in silence and listen as the flames crackle in the fireplace.

Lynn quietly says, "It all changes now, doesn't it? After all these years, it's no longer the John Victor company. Are you OK with that?"

"Yes. It's time. It feels right."

"I'm so proud of what you have accomplished, honey."

"Thanks, babe. I appreciate it."

There is another quiet interlude as they watch the flames.

"So, we need to decide; what's the first place we will visit?" she asks.

"I've always wanted to see Alaska."

"You are aware we are already freezing right here in

Ohio, right?"

"Alright, tell me your first choice."

"Maui. Famous beaches and Pina Coladas."

"That's a long flight. Why couldn't we just go to Florida to escape the cold?"

"Because it's not Maui."

"So, we agree to disagree on that one. Maybe instead, we start our travel with Italy. Say, the Amalfi Coast?"

Lynn thinks for a moment. "That could actually work."

"Really? Let the record reflect we've made a break-through tonight. So, we agree to agree?"

"I agree."

They clink glasses.

ABOUT THE AUTHOR

Bob Fisher's background includes founding and running a technology company for 20 years before having it acquired by a Silicon Valley firm. He has an undergraduate degree in English and Mathematics from Washington University in St. Louis and a graduate degree in Computer Science from Ohio State University. Bob lives with his wife Tina in central Ohio and sometimes in Sarasota Florida.